DECLARATION OF HUMAN RIGHTS

DECLARATION OF HUMAN RIGHTS

Edited by
Dr. S.K. Panneer Selvam
Assistant Professor
Department of Education
Bharathidasan University
Tiruchirappalli
Tamil Nadu
(India)

DISCOVERY PUBLISHING HOUSE PVT. LTD.
NEW DELHI-110 002

Published by:
Tilak Wasan
DISCOVERY PUBLISHING HOUSE PVT. LTD.
4383/4A, Ansari Road, Darya Ganj
New Delhi-110 002 (India)
Phone : +91-11-23279245, 43596064-65
Fax : +91-11-23253475
E-mail : parul.wasan@gmail.com
discoverypublishinghouse@gmail.com
web : www.discoverypublishinggroup.com

First Edition: 2012

ISBN: 978-93-5056-075-4

Declaration of Human Rights

Printed at:
Shree Balaji Art Press
Delhi

PREFACE

UNESCO's commemorative activities were launched by the Director-General on 10 December 2007 during an event at UNESCO Headquarters. Eminent experts from various regions along with a representative of the OHCHR took part in that event. The commemorative activities were concluded, in accordance with 180 EX/Decision 9, by the signature of the Agreement on the Establishment of the International Centre for the Advancement of Human Rights in Buenos Aires, Argentina, on 13 February 2009. The International Coalition of Cities against Racism was created during the third edition of the World Forum of Human Rights in Nantes (France), which was launched at the initiative of and in partnership with UNESCO in 2004. A memorandum of understanding was signed with the City of Bilbao (Spain), which became the donor of the UNESCO/Bilbao Prize for the Promotion of a Culture of Human Rights. The commemoration was also an opportunity to further strengthen interaction with existing partners. Within the United Nations, UNESCO maintained regular contact with the OHCHR throughout the year. The mainstreaming of human rights in UNESCO requires integration of a human rights based approach into all its activities and projects. To reach this goal, capacity-building to increase the knowledge on the part of UNESCO staff of human rights standards, major challenges to human rights and the human rights-based approach to programming should be continued. Activities in the field of human rights and gender equality should be further articulated and their in-house coordination should be further intensified in order to ensure a more effective contribution to the advancement of all human rights, particularly those within UNESCO's competence and ensuring gender equality.

The importance of education and human capital has been brought out in many studies of economic growth and development. Robert (1991) developed a human capital model which shows that education and the creation of human capital was responsible for both the differences in labour productivity and the differences in overall levels of technology that we observe in the world. More than anything else, it has been the spectacular growth in East Asia that has given education and human capital their current popularity in the field of economic growth and development. Countries such as Hong Kong, Korea, Singapore, and Taiwan have achieved unprecedented rates of economic growth while making large investments in education. In the statistical analysis that accompanied his study, the World Bank (1993) found that improvement in education is a very significant explanatory variable for East Asian economic growth. The concept of emotional intelligence has become so popular in the management literature that it has become imperative to understand and leverage it for the sake of enhancing the capacity of human capital in organizations. As the pace of change is increasing and world of work is making ever greater demands on a person's cognitive, emotional and physical resources, this particular set of abilities are becoming increasingly important. Since majority of the concerns in organization involve people in different roles, emotional intelligence must become a determining factor for their effective management. It has also been found that ultimately it is the emotional and personal competencies that we need to identify and measure if we want to be able to predict performance at workplace resulting in its effectiveness, thereby enhancing the worth of the human capital. In this scenario the competencies possessed by the people will have a bearing on the extent to which they can actualize their emotional intelligence. The current paper sets out to examine the relationship between the emotional intelligence of executives in Indian business organizations with their personal competencies. The result suggests that emotional intelligence is significantly related with the personal competencies of employees and the variables of personal competency namely, people success, system success and self success have a predictive relationship with emotional intelligence. The emotional intelligence intervention is partly a response to the problems that businesses face today. There is a need to develop the highest standard of leadership skills, the challenges of high team turnover, ever increasing demands of customers for high quality goods and services, rapidly changing business environment, economic demands or escalating costs. What companies need is people who have both technical knowledge and social and emotional abilities which will enable them to delight the customers. Emotional intelligence can contribute to developing those skills and abilities that are linked with this aspiration (Orme & Langhorn, 2003). Personal competencies play a very vital role in influencing the emotional intelligence of employees in organizations. This edition is mainly a sum total of works and the findings are goes to Olaniyan and Okemakinde, Department *of Educational Management,* University of Ibadan, Ibadan and Kavita Singh, Faculty of Management Studies, University of Delhi and Julie L. Brockman & Antonio A. Nunez & Archana Basu, School of Labour and Industrial Relations at Michigan State University. The originality of this edition owes to the originality of the contributors valuable works. As an editor I acknowledged all the contributors.

Editors

CONTENTS

CHAPTER

Universal Declaration of Human Rights

ABSTRACT

34 C/Resolution 38 invited the Director-General to submit a report to the General Conference at its 35th session on the commemorative activities celebrating the 60th anniversary of the Universal Declaration of Human Rights and on the ways in which those activities specifically advanced the objectives set forth in the plan of action for the commemoration.

Purpose: *The present document informs the General Conference on the above. A list of commemorative activities carried out by UNESCO and its partners is available on request.*

Background

1. The United Nations Secretary-General invited the United Nations system to actively commemorate, in 2008, the 60th anniversary of the Universal Declaration of Human Rights (UDHR), under the motto 'Dignity and Justice for All of Us', under the responsibility of the Office of the United Nations High Commissioner for Human Rights (OHCHR). The General Conference, at its 34th session, discussed elements of a draft UNESCO Plan of Action for the commemoration of the 60th anniversary of the UDHR (34 C/59)

that had been elaborated in consultations with Member States, their National Commissions and Permanent Delegations, as well as with other relevant partners, including human rights NGOs, UNESCO Chairs and human rights research and training institutions. By 34 C/Resolution 38, the General Conference requested the Director-General to further refine UNESCO's plan of action and to report on the progress of commemorative activities to the Executive Board at its 179th session. The Board, by 179 EX/Decision 8, welcomed the Plan. Further progress was reported to the Executive Board at its 180th session.

2. UNESCO's commemorative activities were launched by the Director-General on 10 December 2007 during an event at UNESCO Headquarters. Eminent experts from various regions along with a representative of the OHCHR took part in that event. The commemorative activities were concluded, in accordance with 180 EX/Decision 9, by the signature of the Agreement on the Establishment of the International Centre for the Advancement of Human Rights in Buenos Aires, Argentina, on 13 February 2009.

UNESCO'S CONTRIBUTION : THEMES, ACTIVITIES, PARTNERSHIPS

3. UNESCO's refined plan of action had three main objectives: (*i*) to promote the implementation of human rights within UNESCO's fields of competence; (*ii*) to encourage reflection and exchange on issues linked to the core mandate of the Organization in the field of human rights, including on emerging ethical and social challenges; and (*iii*) to raise awareness about human rights standards and procedures for their promotion and protection. On each of these three themes, UNESCO and its partners organized a great variety of activities, including conferences and workshops, forums of ministers and experts' meetings, film festivals and exhibitions, and issued publications and posters.

4. On the advancement of the rights within UNESCO competence (Part I of the Plan) the following activities could be mentioned:

- the World Press Freedom Day and the adoption of the Maputo Declaration on freedom of expression and empowerment of people (Maputo, Mozambique, May 2008), as well as the adoption of the Doha Declaration on media and dialogue (Doha, Qatar, May 2009);
- the 61st annual DPI/NGO conference entitled 'Reaffirming Human Rights for All: the Universal Declaration at 60' hosted by UNESCO (3-5 September 2008, UNESCO Headquarters);
- the special meeting of the Executive Board dedicated to the 30th anniversary of the procedure laid down in 104 EX/ Decision 3.3 (30 September 2008, UNESCO Headquarters);
- the International High Level Symposium on Freedom of Expression and the exhibition on safety of journalists (29 October 2008, UNESCO Headquarters);
- the 48th session of the International Conference on Education on the theme "Inclusive Education: The Way of the Future" (25-28 November 2008, Geneva, Switzerland);
- the round table on 'Putting Human Rights into Practice: Role of Education' (10 December 2008, UNESCO Headquarters).

5. Meetings and conferences on pressing human rights issues and emerging ethical and social challenges within the mandate of UNESCO were organized dealing with such issues as education for all, cultural diversity, the rights of migrants, the fight against discrimination, gender equality and the struggle against poverty. These included:

- the World Forum on Human Rights (Nantes, France, 30 June to 3 July 2008);
- the regional conference 'Media, Education and Culture of Human Rights' organized by Colombia in collaboration with UNESCO (8-11 September 2008, Cartagena de Indias, Colombia);

- the round table of the Czech Republic on 'Reporting Human Rights through Documentaries' (25 September 2008, UNESCO Headquarters);
- the third International Conference of the National Council for Human Rights of Egypt entitled 'The Universal Declaration of Human Rights 60 years later: between rhetoric and reality' (1-2 December 2008, Cairo, Egypt);
- the round table entitled 'Human Rights and Cultural Diversity' convened by the Non-aligned Movement (3 December 2008, UNESCO Headquarters);
- the round table on human rights held in Kabul, Afghanistan (in two steps, first on 10 December 2008 and then on 21 July 2009);
- the conference on 'Universality of Human Rights and the Haitian Revolution' (Port-au-Prince, Haiti, August 2009);
- the round table on social justice and human rights organized as a follow-up to the commemoration by the Permanent Delegation of the Bolivarian Republic of Venezuela to UNESCO (30 June 2009, UNESCO Headquarters).

6. Several events and activities were aimed at sensitizing the public at large on the message of the Universal Declaration, among which the following could be mentioned:

- the award of the UNESCO/Bilbao Prize for the Promotion of a Culture of Human Rights (10 December 2008, UNESCO Headquarters);
- the exhibition "UNESCO Speaks Out for Human Rights" (2 December 2008 to 27 February 2009, UNESCO Headquarters);
- the translation of the text of the Universal Declaration into indigenous languages in Venezuela and South Africa, conducted with the support of Member States.

7. UNESCO's commemorative activities represent good examples of the Organization's important role in the promotion of

human rights, with emphasis on those within its competence. The list of commemorative activities undertaken by UNESCO and its partners is available under http://www.unesco.org/shs/humanrights/udhr_60anniversary.

8. UNESCO's appeal for participation as wide as possible in the commemoration received a positive response. Member States further reaffirmed their commitment to human rights by organizing numerous events dedicated to the 60th anniversary of the UDHR. These activities mobilized a broad array of traditional and new partners: National Commissions for UNESCO and Permanent Delegations, national authorities, parliamentarians, national human rights institutions, human research and training centers, UNESCO chairs, clubs, associated schools and the academic community, human rights defenders, non-governmental organizations working in the fields of human rights, gender equality, the struggle against all forms of discrimination and poverty, as well as other civil society associations and the media. All these partners worked in close cooperation with UNESCO Headquarters and Field Offices for the realization of many commemorative events.

9. The momentum of the commemoration led to the creation of new partnerships. The end of the year-long campaign was marked by the establishment of the International Centre for the Advancement of Human Rights as a category 2 centre under the auspices of UNESCO (13 February 2009, Buenos Aires, Argentina). The aspirations that fueled the creation of this centre were presented at a round table organized in cooperation with the Permanent Delegation of Argentina to UNESCO on the theme 'Memory and Human Rights', one of the core themes the new centre will be focussing on (14 April 2009, UNESCO Headquarters). In September 2008 UNESCO signed a memorandum of understanding with the European Inter-University Centre for Human Rights and Democratisation (EIUC), which unites more than 40 universities in Europe and is a very important ally in human rights research and education.

10. The International Coalition of Cities against Racism was created during the third edition of the World Forum of Human Rights

in Nantes (France), which was launched at the initiative of and in partnership with UNESCO in 2004. A memorandum of understanding was signed with the City of Bilbao (Spain), which became the donor of the UNESCO/Bilbao Prize for the Promotion of a Culture of Human Rights. The commemoration was also an opportunity to further strengthen interaction with existing partners. Within the United Nations, UNESCO maintained regular contact with the OHCHR throughout the year.

11. Additionally, numerous activities implemented both at Headquarters and in the field within the context of the programme activities envisaged in document 34 C/5 acquired a stronger human rights dimension and were placed under the banner of the 60th anniversary.

KEY MESSAGES, LESSONS LEARNT AND FUTURE PRIORITIES

12. The core message of the commemoration was that the Universal Declaration of Human Rights is as valid today as it was at its adoption 60 years ago. It has become even more pertinent in the face of negative trends and new challenges with which the world is confronted today, including the global economic and financial crises. The principles and norms enshrined in the UDHR, such as respect for the dignity and rights of all human beings, non-discrimination, gender equality, the need to ensure a decent life for everyone, remain the common standard of achievement for all peoples and all nations. The commemoration also highlighted the fact that, while the significance of national and regional particularities and various historical, cultural and religious backgrounds must be borne in mind, the duty of States, regardless of their political, economic and cultural systems, is to promote and protect all human rights and fundamental freedoms. It also reaffirmed the interrelatedness and interdependence of all human rights: civil, cultural, economic, political and social, and their equal importance to ensure a decent life in dignity for everyone.

13. The commemoration of the Declaration confirmed the pertinence of UNESCO's mandate which stipulates that the Organization's main purpose is to "further universal respect for

justice, for the rule of law and for the human rights and fundamental freedoms which are affirmed for the peoples of the world, without distinction of race, sex, language or religion, by the Charter of the United Nations" (Article I). It also reaffirmed the pertinence of UNESCO's Strategy on Human Rights and the Integrated Strategy to Combat Racism, Racial Discrimination, Xenophobia and Related Intolerance, both adopted by the General Conference in 2003, and the relevance of their main lines of action.

14. The commemorative activities underscored the need to pursue efforts for the advancement of the rights within UNESCO's competence, namely, the right to education; the right to freedom of opinion and expression, including the right to seek, receive and impart information; the right to take part in cultural life; and the right to enjoy the benefits of scientific progress and its applications. These rights are becoming ever more important in the light of globalization, unprecedented scientific and technological progress and increasing movement of people. At the same time it became evident that dialogue and reflection on pressing human rights issues, emerging rights and ethical and social challenges should be pursued with greater intensity. The commemoration confirmed or placed new emphasis on such issues as the struggle against poverty, access to water and sanitation, bioethics, protection of cultural diversity and preventive action to cope with climate change. Moreover, it reiterated the strong support of Member States expressed in the 2005 World Summit Outcome document for the mainstreaming of human rights across the United Nations system.

15. The Organization should therefore further intensify its efforts aimed at: (*i*) mainstreaming human rights throughout its programmes; (*ii*) developing human rights research; (*iii*) promoting human rights education; (*iv*) continuing standard-setting and monitoring; and (*v*) further strengthening partnerships.

16. The mainstreaming of human rights in UNESCO requires integration of a human rights based approach into all its activities and projects. To reach this goal, capacity-building to increase the knowledge on the part of UNESCO staff of human rights standards, major challenges to human rights and the human rights-based

approach to programming should be continued. Activities in the field of human rights and gender equality should be further articulated and their in-house coordination should be further intensified in order to ensure a more effective contribution to the advancement of all human rights, particularly those within UNESCO's competence and ensuring gender equality.

17. UNESCO's specific mandate in education, science, culture and communication places the Organization at the forefront of research in order to further elucidate the content of the rights within its competence, namely the right to take part in cultural life and the right to enjoy the benefits of scientific progress and its applications, which are both considered as underdeveloped. In this connection, the Organization will continue its close cooperation with the United Nations Committee on Economic, Social and Cultural Rights. It will also work in concert with the new United Nations Independent Expert in the field of cultural rights. Particular attention will also be paid to emerging ethical and social challenges. UNESCO's long-dated experience in the field of water management and the work of the International Hydrological Programme (IHP) is particularly pertinent to complement the work of the Human Rights Council's newly appointed Independent Expert on the Issue of Human Rights Obligations Related to Access to Safe Drinking Water and Sanitation. Likewise, the identification of obstacles to the implementation of the right to education needs to be particularly emphasized when global economic and financial crises impact negatively on access to education and on its quality, before the specter of rising extremism and intolerance in societies suffering from the lowering standard of living for many of their members. Cooperation with the Independent Expert on the question of human rights and extreme poverty is being developed. UNESCO's work aiming at ensuring the right to freedom of opinion and expression, promoting safety of journalists, fostering free, pluralistic, independent and professional media, advancing media education and applying the Media Development Indicators should be further encouraged.

18. In the area of the struggle against discrimination and racism, the Organization will continue to provide intellectual support and advice to the Regional and International Coalitions of Cities. The

clear support for this initiative voiced by the Durban Review Conference in paragraph 142 of its outcome document demonstrated clearly that working with municipal authorities and local governments constitutes a real niche for UNESCO. It will also pursue its work against HIV/AIDSrelated discrimination through capacity-building and policy-oriented research. In relation to gender equality and women's rights, UNESCO will continue to promote policy-oriented research, *inter alia*, by providing support to the Palestinian Women's Research and Documentation Centre in Ramallah (PWRDC) and the Regional Centre for Research and Documentation on Women to be created in Kinshasa, Democratic Republic of the Congo, covering the Great Lakes region.

19. Ever since the adoption of the UDHR, human rights education has been a priority activity for UNESCO. A first teaching aid produced by UNESCO was published in the early 1950s, and since that time the Organization has always been in the forefront of dissemination of knowledge on human rights and the sensitization of the general public on the problems and challenges in this field. The culture of human rights for which UNESCO has been working for many decades could become a main antidote against intolerance in contemporary societies, which are becoming more and more multilingual, multi-religious and multicultural. Education for memory, which is one of the main tasks of the Centre established in Buenos Aires, is also an important means to establish constructive dialogue and prevent the repetition of the atrocities of the past. Constructive dialogue, together with education, is the most appropriate tool to advance human rights as pursued by the International Year of Human Rights Learning (2009) and the World Programme for Human Rights Education (from 2005 onwards). The participation of UNESCO in the preparation of a draft declaration on human rights education by the United Nations Human Rights Council is particularly important.

20. Strengthened partnerships and cooperation are indispensable. Within the United Nations system, cooperation with the OHCHR and sister agencies will be further developed and

deepened. The same applies to treaty bodies and special procedures mandate holders, as well as to new partners such as the International Centre for the Advancement of Human Rights in Buenos Aires, which should launch its activities in 2010.

21. The momentum gained during the commemoration of the 60th anniversary of the UDHR is a valuable asset and should not be lost. The Organization must build upon its recognized role in the field of human rights and continue its efforts in all its fields of competence in order to make dignity and justice a reality for all.

22. The General Conference may wish to adopt the draft resolution proposed below:

The General Conference, Recalling 34 C/Resolution 38 concerning the celebration of the 60th anniversary of the Universal Declaration of Human Rights, Recognizing that while the significance of national and regional particularities and various historical, cultural and religious backgrounds must be borne in mind, the duty of States, regardless of their political, economic and cultural systems, is to promote and protect all human rights and fundamental freedoms, Reaffirming the interrelatedness and interdependence of all human rights—civil, cultural, economic, political and social—and their equal importance to ensure a decent life in dignity for everyone, Stressing UNESCO's commitment to the promotion of universal respect for and observance of human rights and fundamental freedoms without distinction of race, sex, language or religion in line with its Constitution, the UNESCO Strategy on Human Rights (32 C/Resolution 27), the Integrated Strategy to Combat Racism, Racial Discrimination, Xenophobia and Related Intolerance (32 C/13) and the Medium-Term Strategy for 2008-2013 (34 C/4), Recognizing the increasing importance of the rights within UNESCO's competence, namely the right to education, the right to freedom of opinion and expression, including the right to seek, receive and impart information, the right to take part in cultural life, the right to enjoy the benefits of scientific progress and its applications, in the era of globalization, unprecedented scientific and technological progress and growing movement of people,

Reaffirming UNESCO's commitment to the realization of the internationally agreed development goals, including the Millennium Development Goals, and the need for additional emphasis on the promotion of gender equality—a global priority of UNESCO—and the struggle against poverty, Concerned by the negative impact of global economic and financial crises on the enjoyment of all human rights, in particular those within the UNESCO mandate, Having examined document 35 C/44,

1. Welcomes UNESCO's contribution to the year-long United Nations system-wide campaign to commemorate the 60th anniversary of the Universal Declaration of Human Rights through the activities carried out in the framework of the UNESCO refined plan of action;
2. Commends UNESCO Member States, as well as all traditional and new partners, for their contribution to the commemoration of the 60th anniversary of the Universal Declaration of Human Rights;
3. Recommends that UNESCO intensify human rights activities in line with the UNESCO Strategy on Human Rights and the Integrated Strategy to Combat Racism, Racial Discrimination, Xenophobia and Related Intolerance, both adopted by the General Conference in 2003;
4. Further recommends that efforts be pursued to mainstream human rights into all UNESCO programmes, in particular through training, capacity-building of UNESCO staff and programme reviews with a view to applying a human rights-based approach at all stages of programming, and to submit to the Executive Board at its 185th session a plan on human rights mainstreaming;
5. Invites the Director-General to further promote policy-oriented research and knowledge sharing on the rights within UNESCO's competence, including on the right to access safe drinking water and sanitation, gender equality and women's rights and the struggle against poverty, in full conformity with universal human rights standards;

6. Calls for further development of human rights education both in formal and non-formal settings, sensitization of public opinion on emerging problems in this field and participation in the elaboration of a United Nations normative instrument concerning human rights education;
7. Welcomes efforts to monitor the implementation of UNESCO standard-setting instruments related to human rights and to raise awareness about these instruments and the 104 EX/3.3 procedures;
8. Invites the Director-General to further increase coordination and cooperation in the field of human rights and gender equality with traditional and new partners, in particular with the Office of the High Commissioner for Human Rights, the United Nations treaty bodies, the Human Rights Council and special procedure mandate holders and to undertake, when necessary, steps to institutionalize such cooperation;
9. Urges all public and private institutions within the Member States, civil society, including non-governmental organizations, educational institutions and educators, National Commissions for UNESCO, as well as human rights institutions to build on the momentum created during the commemoration of the 60th anniversary of the UDHR by undertaking activities to further promote and protect human rights and fundamental freedoms particularly at a time of global economic and financial crises;
10. Invites the Director-General to reinforce the implementation of the UNESCO Strategy on Human Rights and the Integrated Strategy to Combat Racism, Racial Discrimination, Xenophobia and Related Intolerance, by taking due account of new priorities and challenges in the area of human rights, notably those deriving from the global economic and financial crises, as well as the achievements and lessons learned from the commemoration of the 60th anniversary of the Universal Declaration, and to present a report thereon to the Executive Board at its 185th session.

CHAPTER

Human Capital Theory
Implications for Educational Development

ABSTRACT

The belief that education is an engine of growth rests on the quality and quantity of education in any country. The paper posits that formal education is highly instrumental and even necessary to improve the production capacity of a nation and discusses the rationality behind investment in human capital. Empirical evidences of human capital model were identified and findings reveal that investment in education has positive correlation with economic growth and development. Criteria for the applicability and problems associated with the theory were identified and implications for educational development highlighted. Conclusively, the paper recommends that for education to contribute significantly to economic growth and development, it must be of high quality to meet the skill-demand needs of the economy.

Introduction

Education is an economic good because it is not easily obtainable and thus needs to be apportioned. Economists regard education as both consumer and capital good because it offers utility to a consumer and also serves as an input into the production of other goods and services. As a capital good, education can be used to develop the human resources necessary for economic and social transformation. The focus on education as a capital good relates to the concept of human capital, which emphasizes that the development of skills is an important factor in production activities. It is widely accepted that education creates improved citizens and helps to upgrade the general standard of living in a society. Therefore, positive social change is likely to be associated with the production of qualitative citizenry. This increasing faith in education as an agent of change in many developing countries, including Nigeria, has led to a heavy investment in it. The pressure for higher education in many developing countries has undoubtedly been helped by public perception of financial reward from pursuing such education. Generally, this goes with the belief that expanding education promotes economic growth.

However, the paradox accompanying this belief is that, despite the huge investment on education, there is little evidence of growth-promoting externalities of education in Nigeria.

Concept of Human Capital Theory

The economic prosperity and functioning of a nation depend on its physical and human capital stock. Whereas the former has traditionally been the focus of economic research, factors affecting the enhancement of human skills and talent are increasingly figuring in the research of social and behavioural sciences. In general terms, human capital represents the investment people make in themselves that enhance their economic productivity.

The theoretical framework most responsible for the wholesome adoption of education and development policies has come to be known as human capital theory. Based upon the work of Schultz (1971), Sakamota and Powers (1995), Psacharopoulos and Woodhall (1997), human capital theory rests on the assumption that formal education is highly instrumental and even necessary to improve the production capacity of a population. In short, the human capital theorists argue that an educated population is a productive population.

Human capital theory emphasizes how education increases the productivity and efficiency of workers by increasing the level of cognitive stock of economically productive human capability which is a product of innate abilities and investment in human beings. The provision of formal education is seen as a productive investment in human capital, which the proponents of the theory have considered as equally or even more equally worthwhile than that of physical capital.

According to Babalola (2003), the rationality behind investment in human capital is based on three arguments:

(*i*) that the new generation must be given the appropriate parts of the knowledge which has already been accumulated by previous generations;

(*ii*) that new generation should be taught how existing knowledge should be used to develop new products, to introduce new processes and production methods and social services; and

(*iii*) that people must be encouraged to develop entirely new ideas, products, processes and methods through creative approaches.

According to Fagerlind and Saha, (1997) human capital theory provides a basic justification for large public expenditure on education both in developing and developed nations. The theory was consistent with the ideologies of democracy and liberal progression found in most Western societies.

Its appeal was based upon the presumed economic return of investment in education both at the macro and micro levels. Efforts to promote investment in human capital were seen to result in rapid economic growth for society. For individuals, such investment was seen to provide returns in the form of individual economic success and achievement.

Most economists agree that it is human resources of nation, not its capital nor its material resources that ultimately determine the character and pace of its economic and social development. Psacharopoulos and Woodhall (1997) assert that:

> *Human resources constitute the ultimate basis of wealth of nations. Capital and natural resources are passive factors of production, human beings are the active agencies who accumulate capital, exploit natural resources, build social, economic and political organization, and carry forward national development. p. 102.*

Empirical Evidence of Human Capital Model

The importance of education and human capital has been brought out in many studies of economic growth and development. Robert (1991) developed a human capital model which shows that education and the creation of human capital was responsible for both the differences in labour productivity and the differences in overall levels of technology that we observe in the world. More than anything else, it has been the spectacular growth in East Asia that has given education and human capital their current popularity in the field of economic growth and development. Countries such as Hong Kong, Korea, Singapore, and Taiwan have achieved unprecedented rates of economic growth while making large investments in education. In the statistical analysis that accompanied his study, the World Bank (1993) found that improvement in education is a very significant explanatory variable for East Asian economic growth.

There are several ways of modeling how the huge expansion of education accelerated economic growth and development. The first is to view education as an investment in human capital. A different view of the role of education in the economic success is that education has positive externalities. "Educate part of the community and the whole of it benefits,". The idea that education generates positive externalities is by no means new. Many of the classical economists argued strongly for government's active support of education on the grounds of the positive externalities that society would gain from a more educated labour force and populace. (Van-

Den-Berg 2001). Smith (1976) reflects such progressive contemporary thought when he wrote that by educating its people, a society:

> *derives no inconsiderable advantage from their instruction. The more they are instructed, the less liable they are to the delusions of enthusiasm and superstition, which, among ignorant nations, frequently occasion the most dreadful disorders. An instructed and intelligent people besides, are always more decent and orderly than an ignorant and stupid ones. p. 68.*

Smith views the externalities to education as important to the proper functioning not only of the economy but of a democratic society. Another way of modeling the role of education in the growth and development process is to view human capital as a critical input for innovations, research and development activities. From this perspective, education is seen as an intentional effort to increase the resources needed for creating new ideas, and thus, any increase in education will directly accelerate technological progress. This modeling approach usually adopts the Schumpeter (1973) assumptions of imperfectly competitive product markets and competitive innovation, which permit the process of generating technological progress. Education is seen as an input into the intentional and entrepreneurial efforts to create new technology and new products. Proponents of this view of education point out the close correlation between new product development and levels of education. The countries that are at the forefront of technology also have the most educated population (Van-Den-Berg 2001).

The review of empirical tests of the theory by Garba (2002) shows that cross-country regressions have shown positive correlation between educational attainment and economic growth and development. Odekunle (2001) affirms that investment in human capital has positive effects on the supply of entrepreneurial activity and technological innovation. Ayeni (2003) asserts that education as an investment has future benefits of creation of status, job security and other benefits in cash and in kind.

However, Ayara (2002) reports that education has not had the expected positive growth impact on economic growth in Nigeria. Hence, he proposes three possibilities that could account for such results, which are:

(*i*) Educational capital has gone into privately remunerative but socially unproductive activities; or

(*ii*) There has been slow growth in the demand for educated labour; or

(*iii*) The education system has failed, such that schooling provides few (or no) skills.

Application of Human Capital Theory to Educational System

Babalola (2003) asserts that the contribution of education to economic growth and development occurs through its ability to increase the productivity of an existing labour force in various ways. However, economic evaluation of educational investment projects should take into account certain criteria according to Psacharopoulos and Woodhall (1997) which are:

- Direct economic returns to investment, in terms of the balance between the opportunity costs of resources and the expected future benefits;
- Indirect economic returns, in terms of external benefits affecting other members of society; Human Capital Theory: Implications for Educational Development 160
- The private demand for education and other factors determining individual demand for education;
- The geographical and social distribution of educational opportunities; and,
- The distribution of financial benefits and burdens of education.

Education plays a great and significant role in the economy of a nation, thus educational expenditures are found to constitute a form of investment. This augments individual's human capital and leads to greater output for society and enhanced earnings for the individual worker. It increases their chances of employment in the labour market, and allows them to reap pecuniary and nonpecuniary returns and gives them opportunities for job mobility. Education is a source of economic growth and development only if it is anti-traditional to the extent that it liberates, stimulates and informs the individual and teaches him how and why to make demands upon himself. Accordingly, a proper educational strategy would manifest itself in four major development-producing capacities. According to Bronchi (2003) the first is the development of a general trend favourable to economic progress. The reference is to social mobility, a general increase in literacy necessary for improved communication.

The second capacity emphasizes the development of complementary resources for factors which are relatively plenty and substitutes for relatively scarce factors. That is, educated people would be more adaptable to varying production needs. The third capacity underscores the durability of educational investment. He argues that education has greater durability than most forms of non-human reproductive capital, which implies that a given investment in education tends to be more productive, other things being equal, than some outlay on non-human capital. Finally, education is an alternative to consumption, for it transfers to round-about production the resources that would otherwise be consumed now.

Sensitivity of Human Capital Theory

The main problem associated with the belief that education is good for economic growth and development according to Babalola (2003) concerns how to maintain an equilibrium position. That is, where there will be no evidence of either shortage or surplus supply of educated people. A shortage of educated people might limit growth, while excess supply of it might create unemployment and thus limit economic growth and development. The theory has been criticized on several grounds. At the individual level, it has become controversial whether or to what extent education or other forms of human investments are directly related to improvement in occupation and income. Bronchi (2003) asserts that raising the level of education in a society can under certain instances increase the inequalities in income distribution.

Fagerlind and Saha (1997) assert that while governments may adopt educational plans consistent with specific development goals and strategies, they can only be partially certain that outcomes of these will correspond to original intentions; the more political the goals of education, the more problematic the outcomes. In light of this, to view education as a panacea for the attainment of development objectives is risky. Thus, education in general and schooling in particular, cannot of its own achieve the desired societal goals without structural reforms. Another major problem in the application of the theory is its failure to account for a growing gap between people's increasing learning efforts and knowledge base and the diminishing number of commensurate jobs to apply their increasing knowledge investment, especially in developing nations.

To this, some advocates of the theory (Bronchi, 2003, Castronova 2002, Crepaz and Moser 2004) assert that these great increases in learning efforts have not led to commensurate economic gains because of the declining quality of education, lopsided and politically motivated system of education.

Implications of Human Capital Theory for Educational Development

The central difference in the policy implications of the human capital model and the alternative models relates to the desirable level of public expenditure on education. The basic implication of the human capital model is that allocation of resources on education should be expanded to the point where the present value of the streams of returns to marginal investment is equal or greater than the marginal costs.

Many of the developing nations have thus realized that the principal mechanism for developing human knowledge is the education system. Thus, they invest huge sum of money on education not only as an attempt to impact knowledge and skills to individuals but also to impart values, ideas, attitudes and aspirations which may be in the nation's best developmental interest.

In addition to manpower planning needs, parents strongly feel that in an era of scarce skilled manpower, the better the education their children can get, the better are their chances of getting well paid jobs. The poor often look at their children's education as the best means of escaping poverty. The concept of human resources has provided a useful bridge between the theoretical concerns of students of the developmental process and the practical requirements of assistance to planners.

Irrespective of the explanation given for global educational expansion, the consequences of this expansion for social systems can be problematic. The tensions and strains of educational expansion can impede economic, social and political development. For example, the accelerated costs of expanding educational system compete with other sectors of the respective societies for finite resources. As mass primary education is attained, expansion shifts to the secondary and tertiary levels as these too are gradually transformed into mass systems. At the same time, the increase in costs is not arithmetic but geometric. These pressures ultimately create dilemma for government who must realistically assess and determine spending priorities for scarce economic resources.

Adopting a position based on the assumptions of the human capital and modernization theorists, Fagerlind and Saha (1997) argue that in developing countries at least, educational demand must be tempered in order to bring costs and benefits to more realistic levels.

Among the suggestions they made are that:

- The costs of education should be borne by the beneficiary or recipient by means of family assistance or self-help schemes rather than solely the state;
- The income differential between the traditional and modern sectors should be reduced, which in effect lowers the benefits according to the educational attainments;

- The educational requirements for particular jobs should not be exaggerated; and
- The wage structure should be tied to occupational and requirements rather than educational attainments.

It is also worth noting that the causal relationship between education and earnings has important implications for public policy. If human capital theorists are correct in arguing that education is the primary cause of higher earnings, then it obviously makes sense to provide more education to low-income groups of society to reduce poverty and the degree of income inequality. This analysis suggests that the primary focus of subsidies to education should be on ensuring that all those who can benefit from, have access to appropriate opportunities, rather than on reducing costs incurred by those who would undertake higher education in any case.

Conclusion and Recommendations

Nigeria is confronted by most of the problems that could limit the capacity of expansion in education to stimulate growth and development such as under-employment, low absorptive capacity, shortage of professionals, regional imbalances and brain-drain. The persistence of many of the problems in spite of the various policy formulation and responses points to the need for a more focused, responsive, functional and qualitative educational system. To contribute significantly to economic growth and development, education must be of high quality and also meet the skill-demand needs of the economy.

It is not a noble achievement for any sector of the economy to exist for years only to make a negligible contribution to economic growth, which is not commensurate with its life span and investment. In this case, there is the need for more commitment by the authorities not to interfere with decisions such as curriculum or teachers' responsibilities. Parents should not wish to fulfill their life expectations in their children by selecting careers for them or by suggesting subjects that they should study. They should not also encourage or assist their children and wards to purchase certificates.

Government, in its employment policies, should lay more emphasis on specialization and competence rather than paper qualification and ill-gotten certificates.

REFERENCES

1. Ayara, N. N (2002) The Paradox of Education and Economic Growth in Nigeria: Empirical Evidence. *Selected papers for the 2002 Annual Conference*. Nigerian Economic Society (NES) Ibadan. Polygraphics Ventures Ltd.
2. Ayeni, O. (2003) Relationship Between Training and Employment of Technical College Graduates in Oyo State between 1998 and 2001. *Unpublished Ph.D Thesis*. University of Ibadan, Ibadan.
3. Babalola, J.B. (2003) Budget Preparation and Expenditure Control in Education. In Babalola J.B. (ed) *Basic Text in Educational Planning*. Ibadan Awemark Industrial Printers.
4. Bronchi, C. (2003); The Effectiveness of Public Expenditure in Portugal; *Economics Department Working Paper 349*; OECD.
5. Castronova, E. (2002); To Aid, Insure, Transfer or Control—What Drives the Welfare State?; DIW Berlin; *German Institute for Economic Research; Discussion Paper 281*.
6. Crepaz, M. and A. Moser (2004); The Impact of Collective and Competitive Veto Points on Public Expenditures in the Global Age; *Comparative Political Studies*; 37; (6) pp. 259-285.
7. Fagerlind, A. and Saha, L.J. (1997) *Education and National Developments*. New Delhi. Reed Educational and Professional Publishing Ltd.
8. Garba, P.K (2002) Human Capital Formation, Utilization and the Development of Nigeria. *Selected Papers for the 2002 Annual Conference of the Nigeria Economic Society*. (NES). Ibadan. Polygraphics Ventures Ltd.
9. Odekunle, S.O. (2001) Training and Skill Development as Determinant of Workers' Productivity in the Oyo State Public Service. *Unpublished Ph.D Thesis*, University of Ibadan.
10. Psacharopoulos, G and Woodhall, M. (1997) *Education for Development—An Analysis of Investment Choice*. New York Oxford University Press.
11. Robert, B. (1991) Economic Growth in a Cross Section of Countries. *Quarterly Journal of Economic* 106 (2) p. 407-414.

12. Sakamota, A. and Powers, P.A. (1995) Education and the Dual Labour Market for Japanaese men in America. *Sociological Review*. 60 (2) P. 222-246.
13. Schultz, T.W. (1971) *Investment in Human Capital*. New York. The Free Press.
14. Schumpeter, J. (1973) *The Theory of Economic Development*. Cambridge, Mass: Harvar University Press.
15. Smith, A. (1976) *An Inquiry into the Nature and Causes of Wealth of Nations*. Chicago University of Chicago Press.
16. Van-Den-Berg, H. (2001) *Economic Growth and Development* (International Edition) New York. McGraw-Hill Companies, Inc.
17. *World Bank* (1995) Review of Public Expenditure ODI, London.

CHAPTER

Developing Human Capital

Linking Emotional Intelligence with Personal Competencies in Indian Business Organizations

Introduction

James Dozier discovered the power of emotional intelligence in 1981, which resulted in saving his life. Dozier was a U.S. Army Brigadier General who was kidnapped by the Red Brigades, an Italian terrorist group. During the initial days his captives were euphoric with excitement and were agitated and irrational at times and he felt that his life was in danger. To save himself, he remembered something he had learned about emotion in an Executive Development Programme at the Centre for Creative Leadership in Greensboro, North Carolina.

Emotions are contagious, and a single person can influence the emotional tone of a group by modelling. He first thought of getting his own emotions under control, quite a difficult task to achieve! He tried to calm himself and conveyed his calmness to his captives through his actions. He then realized that his captors also caught his calmness and became more rational. In retrospect when Dozier looked back on this episode, he was convinced that his ability to manage his own emotional reactions and those of his captors literally saved his life (Campbell, 1990).

The term emotional intelligence (EI) had not been coined in 1981, but James Dozier actually experienced it live and gave us an initial framework to identify what it is: "The ability to perceive and express emotion, assimilate emotion in thought, understand and reason with emotion, and regulate emotion in the self and others" (Mayer, Salovey, & Caruso 2000). Dozier could perceive accurately the emotional reactions of his captors, and he also diagnosed the danger that those reactions posed for him. By regulating his emotions and then expressing them effectively, he was able to manage the emotions of his captors. This incident illustrates emotional intelligence in action.

Since then the concept of emotional intelligence has become so popular in the management literature that it has become imperative to understand and be aware of the research and theory on which it is based. It is also useful to consider how emotional intelligence is important for effective performance at work place. As the pace of change is increasing and world of work is making ever greater demands on a person s cognitive, emotional and physical resources, this particular set of abilities are becoming increasingly important.

Traditional measures of intelligence, although providing some degree of predictive validity, have not been able to account for a large portion of the variance in work performance and career success. As Goleman (1998) states, "When IQ test scores are correlated with how well people perform in their careers the highest estimate of how much difference IQ accounts for is about 25 per cent (Hunter & Hunter, 1984; Schmidt & Hunter, 1981). A careful analysis, though, suggests that a more accurate figure may be no higher than 10 per cent and perhaps as low as 4 per cent" (Sternberg, 1997).

The Impact of Emotional Intelligence on Workplace Effectiveness

Look deeply at almost any factor that influences work place effectiveness, and you will find that emotional intelligence plays a role. Any growing and prosperous organization needs to retain good employees, particularly those with the competencies that are important in the high-tech economy. What is it that can make an employee stay with an organization for a longer duration? A Gallup Organization study of two million employees at seven hundred companies found that duration of stay of an employee in a company and his productivity would be determined by his relationship with his immediate supervisor (Zipkin, 2000). In another study by Spherion, a staffing and consulting firm in Fort Lauderdale, Florida, and Lou Harris Associates, it was found that only 11 per cent of the employees who ranked their bosses as excellent were likely to look for another job, however, 40 per cent of those who ranked their bosses as poor wanted to leave. In other words, people who have good relation with boss are four times less likely to leave than are those who have poor relationship (Zipkin, 2000).

The greatest challenges that the organizations face today include (Cherniss, 2001):

- Coping with massive, rapid change.
- Employees need to be more creative in order to drive innovation.
- Managing huge amounts of information.
- Enhancing customer loyalty.
- Employees need to be more motivated and committed.
- Need for collaborative effort.
- The organization needs to make better use of the special talents available in a diverse workforce.
- The organization needs to identify potential leaders in its ranks and prepare them to move up.
- The organization needs to identify and recruit top talent.
- The organization needs to make good decisions about new markets, products, and strategic alliances.
- The organization needs to prepare employees for overseas assignments.

These and many more concerns today confront work organizations, both public and private. Since majority of these concerns involve people in different roles, emotional intelligence must become a determining factor for their effective management. And in virtually every case, emotional intelligence must play an important role in handling the concern. For instance, while dealing with the process of change in an organization a lot of emotions get generated which may range from very positive to very negative (Singh, 2005). This requires ability on the part of both the employer and the employees to perceive and understand the emotional impact of change on self and others. To be effective in helping their organizations manage change, leaders should be aware of and manage feelings of anxiety and uncertainty of their employees (Bunker, 1997). They also should be able to appreciate the emotional reactions of other employees and help them to cope up with change. Besides the leader, the other members of the organization should be also able to monitor and manage their own emotional reaction as well as of their colleagues. Ultimately it is these social and emotional competencies that we need to identify and measure if we want to be able to predict performance at workplace resulting in its effectiveness.

LITERATURE REVIEW

Emotional Intelligence

Salovey and Mayer (1990) coined the term emotional intelligence in 1990, while being aware of the previous work on non-cognitive aspects of intelligence. They described emotional intelligence as "a form of social intelligence that involves the ability to monitor one's own and others feelings and emotions, to discriminate among them, and to use this information to guide one's thinking and action". In the early 1990 s Daniel Goleman became aware of Salovey and Mayer's work, and this eventually led to his book on Emotional Intelligence.

Goleman proposes that cognitive skill 'can help you get a job' in a company, but emotional skill helps you grow in the job once you're hired. To illustrate Goldman's point, psychologist Stein and Book (2006), marketers of tests that assess employees emotional intelligence quotient (EQ), cite the example of a Harvard business graduate who received numerous job offers from companies clamoring to hire her. However, due to a lack of emotional intelligence, the woman continually sparred with her employers and couldn't keep any of the jobs. Goleman (1998) concludes by stating that 'Emotional intelligence matters twice as much as technical and analytic skill combined for star performances. And the higher people move up in the company, the more crucial emotional intelligence becomes.'

To rise higher in one's professional competence at the workplace, it is not just essential that individuals are good in their jobs. They are required to be more positive, approachable, warm, empathetic and optimistic. A number of studies in the area suggest that it takes more than traditional cognitive intelligence to be successful at work. The emotional intelligence of the person which include his ability to restrain the negative feelings and focus on positive feelings plays an important role in determining his success The idea got further boost with the release of a book by Daniel Goleman, 'Emotional Intelligence: Why it Can Matter More than IQ,' (1995).

In another book, 'Working With Emotional Intelligence', Goleman (1998) focused on the need for emotional intelligence at work, an area often considered more head than heart. The notion does not remain limited to the managers and leaders of the organization but any job that requires dealing with people would require the input of emotional intelligence. Also, whereas IQ is relatively fixed, emotional intelligence can be built and learned. Companies can test and teach emotional intelligence, and many employers are already beginning to do so.

For the purpose of the present study, emotional intelligence has been discussed with the help of following dimensions:

***Self Awareness*:** Self-awareness is being conscious of and being able to connect with our personal feelings, thoughts and actions. This helps a person get a clearer perception of what he wants to achieve in life and therefore be able to work on his level of competencies. Self-awareness may also include some degree of self-disclosure so that we can develop effective relationship with other people around us and lead a more fulfilling life by sharing and receiving information.

***Commitment*:** True commitment is a virtue and a personal trait that is learned very early in life. Being committed is a state of mind and is determined by number of factors. It is based on one's own personal choices as well as the expectations from other people around us. It is also determined by the quality of relationship we share with people, groups, organizations or tasks that we are supposed to be committed to be.

***Resilience*:** Resilience refers to one's ability to adjust well in adverse stressful and crises situations. It is the ability to perform well and consistently in a range of situations and when under pressure. The degree of resilience can vary amongst individuals from being high to low on resilience. A number of factors determine a person s ability to be resilient even in adversities. These include age, gender, and frequent exposure to stressful situations.

***Optimism*:** Optimism is defined as an approach in life where a person has a positive belief that good things will happen independent of one's ability. It could be the result of both the inherited characteristics as well as experience. Some of us are naturally inclined to be positive thinkers and therefore optimistic while few of us also acquire it through social interaction. Companies, as well as individuals, create their own internal expectations of optimism or pessimism. The attitude starts with the basic belief in things around us—good or bad.

***Compassion*:** Compassion has been defined as awareness about the suffering of others and a desire to relieve that suffering. It is a kind of emotion: a feeling in motion. In addition to the wish to help the other person in distress it may also involve taking actions and making efforts to help them overcome it. It is an active feeling. When a feeling is active, it can be used as a tool. As a tool, it can be used in a positive or negative manner.

***Interpersonal Connectivity*:** Interpersonal connectivity can be described as an ability to develop effective relationship with other people around you and get along with them both in personal and professional lives. The success of this connectivity would be determined by the response from the other party.

***Personal Integrity*:** Personal integrity refers to a quality of a person's character. This includes being honest with oneself as well as with others around you. It also involves being responsible for what you seek and undertake in life and being able to own up one's own faults in cases of failure. It encompasses the concept of wholeness, intactness and purity about one's thoughts, feelings and actions.

***Emotional Regulation*:** Emotional regulation is the ability to regulate one's emotions whenever required. It may be required to either enhance or reduce one's emotion according to the demands of the situation. Emotional regulation can also be described as a range of skills that are instrumental in keeping the emotional system healthy and functioning. It includes being able to recognize the emotional response and understand it; accept the response as being your own; identify strategies to reduce or enhance the intensity of the emotions; and engage in the goal directed behaviour.

PERSONAL COMPETENCIES

According to Boyatzis (1982), competence means different things to different people. However, it is generally accepted as encompassing knowledge, skills, attitudes and behaviours that are causally related to superior job performance. This understanding of competence can be either described on the basis of attribute-based inference (Gonczi & Hager, 1992) or on the basis of performance-based approach which demonstrates performance at pre-defined acceptable standards in the workplace (Gonczi *et al.,* 1990).

The definition of 'competency' adopted from Parry's (1998) work includes a multi-dimensional approach to understand competency. According to this definition competency:

- is "a cluster of related knowledge, attitudes, skills, and other personal characteristics that affects a major part of one's job;
- correlates with performance on the job;
- can be measured against well-accepted standards;
- can be improved via training and development; and
- can be broken down into different components".

The major components of competencies include: abilities, attitudes, behaviour, knowledge, personality and skills. Another definition of 'personal competency' which has been adopted from Finn (1993) and Crawford (1997) states that personal competency is "the core personality characteristics underlying a person's capability to do a project. These are behaviour, motives, traits, attitudes, and self concepts that enable a person to successfully manage a project". According to Spencer and Spencer (1993) the six components of competency are:

- *Achievement and action*: This competency consists of achievement orientation; concern for order in quality and accuracy; initiative and information seeking.
- *Helping and human service*: This competency implies that the manager has customer service orientation and interpersonal understanding.
- *Impact and influence*: This competency comprises impact and influence capability; organisation awareness and relationship building.
- *Managerial competency*: This competency includes teamwork and cooperation; capability in developing others; team leadership and directiveness, assertiveness and positional power using.
- *Cognitive*: This competency implies that the manager has both analytical thinking capability and conceptual thinking ability.

- *Personal effectiveness*: This competency covers self-control; self-confidence; flexibility and organizational commitment.

Considering the understanding of a number of corporate giants, such as, AT & T, Chevron, Citicorp, General Electric, Honeywell and Pepsi-co, Ryback (1998) has proposed seven core competencies of today's successful managers:

- Strategic planning
- Communication and alignment
- Team building
- Continuous learning
- Dynamic accountability
- Systematic results
- Actualized integrity

LINK BETWEEN EMOTIONAL INTELLIGENCE AND PERSONAL COMPETENCIES

As a person makes a transition from the transactional to transformational approach to create a necessary socio-emotional nearness with people around him, the trait of emotional intelligence becomes a reality. The resultant strengthening of bonds between the individuals help both parties to establish trust and mutuality based on common interests, goals, and a sense of mission, creating the necessary conditions for achievement of personal and organizational goals. Essentially, in order to connect the individual has to bring into play certain personal, social and organizational competencies in mutually acceptable combinations for achieving organizational excellence. Thus, emotionally intelligent behaviour addresses the basic issues for bringing workplace effectiveness and helps to attain higher levels of organizational growth and excellence. This essentially aids in the process of developing congenial work environment in the organization leading to efficiency at the workplace and development and enhancement of human capital.

Recently, some of the American companies have started concentrating on this dimension of the human being. It deals with those ultimate human capacities and potentialities, which have a significant impact on the various aspects of organizational climate. Enrichment of the emotional dimension would help to solve behavioural problems arising from material and social dimensions and contribute to the true effectiveness of an organization (Elankumaran *et.al.,* 2005).

With the opening up of the Indian economy through liberalization, privatization, globalization and natural thrust towards information technology the tasks of Indian business executives has become more demanding. The challenges get multiplied when the Indian executives have to work in diversified work cultures. The workforce diversity has not only offered the emotional stability to the executives but has also come on the way of leadership behaviour and effectiveness (Punia, 2004). Technology represents only 5 per cent of the transformation process; the other 95 per cent of a company's metamorphosis is represented by the changes in organizational behaviour and culture that are the heart of leadership.

The emotional intelligence intervention is partly a response to the problems that businesses face today. There is a need to develop the highest standard of leadership skills, the challenges of high team turnover, ever increasing demands of customers for high quality goods and services, rapidly changing business environment, economic demands or escalating costs. What companies need is people who have both technical knowledge and social and emotional abilities which will enable them to delight the customers. Emotional intelligence can contribute to developing those skills and abilities that are linked with this aspiration (Orme & Langhorn, 2003). Personal competencies play a very vital role in influencing the emotional intelligence of employees in organizations. For the purpose of present study following four dimensions of personal competencies have been identified:

- People success
- Task success

- System success
- Self success

***People Success*:** This competency involves understanding behaviour in interpersonal context, where people refer to connectivity and building bridges with others for attaining and maximizing common goals. Interactivity denotes interrelationship among people and refers to how they relate to one another. Empathy, service and organizational awareness are corner stones of social connectivity. Emotional intelligence is becoming crucial in the context of individual's behaviour within the organizational context. With the flattening of the organization structure, the span of control is now larger for the leader who has to adapt emotionally intelligent behaviour to generate people success. In a study by Singh (2007), it was found that the relationship dimension of individual behaviour is important to be effective leader and adds to his success. Jordan and Troth (2004) also found that emotional intelligence was directly related to performance at group level and emotions are important contributing directly to team performance. Thus the following hypothesis is proposed:

Hypothesis—1: *Emotional intelligence is significantly related to people success.*

***Task Success*:** This competency refers to the ability of the individual to focus on the current task in hand and try to do it with utmost efficiency and accuracy. This will also involve the use of creative thoughts and innovative principles in handling the tasks more effectively. In a study by Lyons and Schneider (2005), it was found that certain dimensions of emotional intelligence were related to more challenge and enhanced performance, thereby increasing task success. Lopes *et. al.,* (2006) found that employees high on emotional intelligence received greater merit increases and held higher company rank than their counterparts. These employees also received better peer and/or supervisor ratings of interpersonal facilitation and stress tolerance. A study by Jaeger (2003) revealed a strong relationship between emotional intelligence and performance of employees leading to task success. On the basis of these findings the following hypothesis is proposed:

Hypothesis—2: *There is a significant positive relationship between Emotional intelligence and task success*

***System Success*:** With this competency, individuals are focused on the organizational issues and the act of doing things together in the organizational context becomes a reality. The following processes occur with this competency in the organizations:

- The person identifies the organizational and environmental variables that control his or her behavior;
- The person works with others to discover the personalized set of environmental or organizational contingencies that regulate their behaviour; and
- The individuals jointly attempt to build bonds to cultivate and maintain a web of relationships to produce more mutually reinforcing and organizationally productive outcomes.

Sy, Tram and O'Hara (2006) reported managers' emotional intelligence had a stronger positive correlation with job satisfaction and job performance. Lyons and Schneider (2005) found that high emotional intelligence levels promote challenge appraisal and lead to better performance. It has been suggested in one of the studies that a link between the emotional intelligence and work place measure of effectiveness would lead to enhanced system success (Rosete & Ciarrochi, 2005). Thus the following hypothesis is proposed:

Hypothesis—3: *Emotional intelligence has a significant positive relationship with system success*

***Self Success*:** This competency consists of self-awareness, which is the basic foundation on which emotionally intelligent behaviour germinates and refers to the ability to read one's own emotions and recognizing their impact to guide decisions. It is necessary for the individuals to have an accurate self assessment by knowing his/her own strengths and limitations (Self directed learning). A self directed learning leads to a positive evaluation of one's self worth and capabilities which are vital for one's success.

Since emotional intelligence comprises both intra-personal and interpersonal abilities, the success of self is the key component of emotional intelligence. Stein and Book (2006) elaborated the concept of self as the ability to recognize one's feelings and to be able to differentiate between them, to know what you are feeling and also to know what caused that feeling. An emotionally intelligent person is able to do thereby leading to self success. Thus the following hypothesis is proposed:

Hypothesis—4: *Emotional intelligence is significantly related to self success.*

For the competencies to be effectively converted into developing an empowered workforce, the following steps are necessary to create an environment in which people can grow:

- Focus on development should be well-communicated;
- Individual should own up the responsibility for their own development and leaders should help them in providing with resources and support;
- After an assessment of the strengths and weaknesses and therefore on the basis of competency gaps, individuals should be able to develop their development plans;
- A deadline should be formulated to achieve the targets with proper feedback system in place; and
- A proper reward system needs to be developed to keep the employees of the organization motivated.

CONCEPTUAL FRAMEWORK

The present study intends to determine the relevance of the concept of emotional intelligence to the business organizations and to explore the extent to which it may be possible to utilize this concept as a means of creating a sustainable competitive advantage by attracting, motivating, training and retaining customer conscious employees at all levels of the organization.

The objective of the study is to develop a framework to identify the relationship between emotional intelligence and personal competencies of executives in Indian business organizations. The expected linkage between the dimensions of personal competencies and emotional intelligence are presented in Figure 3.1. The model in the figure below depicts the influence of personal competencies on emotional intelligent behaviour which is instrumental in enhancing the human capital in this emerging paradigm. In this theoretical construct the dimensions of personal competencies are the independent variables and emotional intelligence is the dependent variable. The model proposes to suggest that to develop an emotionally intelligent work force; personal competencies need to be promoted in business organizations.

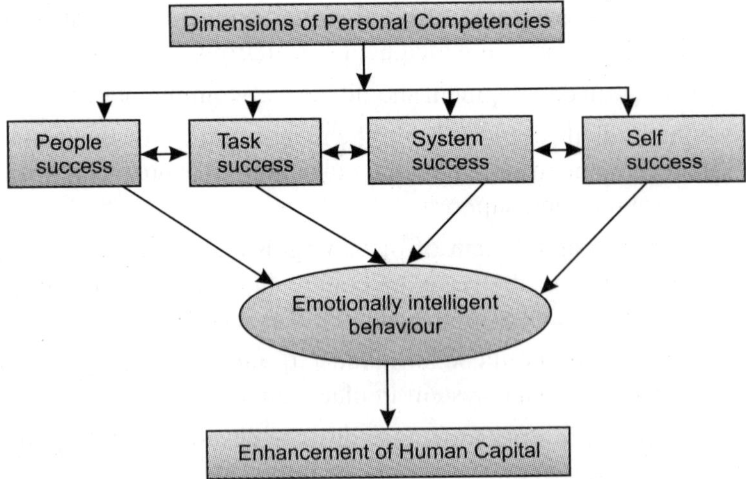

Fig. 3.1 Relationship between Personal Competencies and Emotionally Intelligent Behaviour

METHOD

This section discusses sample size, data collection along with suitable statistical tests used for evaluating research hypotheses.

Sample and Data Collection

A total of 500 self-administered questionnaires were distributed at managerial level. Against the targeted sample of 500 questionnaires,

378 questionnaires have been collected and analyzed. Stratified random sampling was used to collect the data. The distribution of the questionnaire was done on the basis of suitability mostly by personal contact, e-mail and use of postal services. The concerned person was contacted through phone or email before sending the questionnaire. As the questionnaire was self explanatory, the respondents were asked to respond as per the instructions given in the questionnaire and were assured of confidentiality. A total of 378 correctly completed questionnaire were returned by the respondents.

There were three sections of the questionnaire used to collect the necessary data. The *first* portion of the questionnaire inquired about the personal information of the respondents. The *second* portion focussed on emotional intelligence (dependent variable) and consisted of 8 dimensions measured with the help of 40 items with the highest score being 200. The eight dimensions were:

1. Self awareness
2. Commitment
3. Resilience
4. Optimism
5. Compassion
6. Interpersonal Connectivity
7. Personal Integrity
8. Emotional Regulation

The scales used in the questionnaire included the Likert Scale. The Likert scale uses a rating of 1 to 5, where 1 indicates 'Strongly Disagree' and 5 indicates 'Strongly Agree'. The reliability statistics Cronbach Alpha was calculated to be 0.81 for the items. The *third* section of the questionnaire focussed on personal competencies consisting of four dimensions spread over 20 items (measured on a five point scale). This has been developed on the basis of the personal competencies assessment developed by Axiometrics International, Inc. and Workforce Solutions, Inc. It measures four different competencies of the employees namely:

1. People Success
2. Task Success
3. System Success
4. Self Success

The scales used in the questionnaire included the Likert Scale. The Likert scale uses a rating of 1 to 5, where 1 indicates, Strongly Disagree and 5 indicates, Strongly Agree, with the highest score in each of the competencies being 25. The reliability statistics Cronbach Alpha was calculated to be 0.79 for the items.

Analyses of the Data

The data was subjected to statistical analysis for the purpose of interpretation. Descriptive statistics such as mean, standard deviation and intercorrelations were computed to understand the interdependence between the variables. Multiple regression analysis was used to test the hypotheses.

While collecting the data it was observed that there was non-willingness on the part of the executives to participate in the study for the fear of being quoted and identified. Since the study was based on self reported data, so the findings may be biased by common method variance and spurious cause/effect inferences. The generalizations occurring from the study are more conducive and limited to a particular group of employees who participated in the study. It other words, the limitations come from the sampling techniques used, which is non-probability based convenience sampling.

RESULTS

Profile of the Respondents

The total sample size was 378. The group comprised of 102 (27%) females and 276 (73%) males. In the group 26 per cent respondents were in the age group of 21-25 years. 32 per cent of the respondents were in the 26-30 years age category and 22 per cent were in 31-35 years of age. Rest of the respondents were more than 35 years of age. 53 per cent of the respondents were married. While drawing the experience profile of the respondents it was seen that 70 per cent of them had an experience of 5-15 years, followed by 25 per cent with an experience of less than 5 years. 5 per cent were found to be having an experience of 15.25 years. The data was collected from Indian organizations which were situated in and around Delhi, the National Capital of India.

Relationship between the Variables

The following table (Table 3.1) depicts the mean scores and the standard deviations of the variables under study.

Table 3.1 Mean and Standard Deviation of the Variables under Study

S.No.	Variables	Mean score	Standard deviation	Total number of respondents
1.	Emotional Intelligence	152.21 (200)	11.32	378
2.	People Success	20.63 (25)	2.04	378
3.	Task Success	20.35 (25)	2.38	378
4.	System Success	20.48 (25)	2.17	378
5.	Self Success	20.17 (25)	2.08	378

From the above Table 3.1 it can be observed that the emotional intelligence and the competency level of the employees shows a higher score on the mean indicating that executives in business organization generally possess a high level of personal competency and emotional intelligence. The next step in the study is to find out the relationship between the emotional intelligence and the dimensions of personal competencies.

The correlation matrix in Table 3.2 shows the correlation coefficient between the independent variables as identified for the research. A correlation coefficient indicates the strength of the association between the variables. A correlation coefficient is considered significant if the *p*-value is less than 0.05. As shown in

Table 3.2, in the Indian Business organizations all the dimensions of personal competencies like people success, task success, system success and self success have a significant positive relationship with emotional intelligence.

It is observed that system success has the highest correlation with emotional intelligence followed by people success indicating that both have a strong association with emotional intelligence. The next highest is task success followed by self success. The above findings can help us to conclude that employees in Indian organizations perceived that the focus on personal competencies in organizations will be favourable for the existence and sustenance of emotional intelligence.

Table 3.2 Correlation between Emotional Intelligence and the Dimensions of Personal Competencies

S.No.	Variables	1	2	3	4
1.	People Success	—	—	—	—
2.	Task Success	0.262**	—	—	—
3.	System Success	0.290**	0.450**	—	—
4.	Self Success	0.336**	0.366**	0.157**	—
5.	Emotional untelligence	0.480**	0.375**	0.516**	0.360##

**Correlation is significant at the 0.01 level, *Correlation is significant at the 0.05 level

Multiple Regression Analysis

To gain an insight into the relationships further between the independent and dependent variables and to identify the predictive relationships between the two sets of variables, if any, multiple regression analysis was done.

From the correlation tables it can be seen that there are a many significant linear correlation between the emotional intelligence and the constructs of personal competencies. Multiple regression analysis was used to diagnose the relationship between a single dependent variable (criterion) and a number of independent variables (predictors). A set of independent variables is weighted to develop the regression equation or model to explain its relative contribution towards one dependent variable. The dimensions of personal competencies were entered in the model as independent variables, while the emotional intelligence was the dependent variable. The results are depicted in Table 3.3.

Table 3.3 Results of Regression Analysis

S.No.	Independent variables	Coefficient	t	p-value
1.	People Success	0.298	6.906	.000*
2.	Task Success	0.064	1.367	.172
3.	System Success	0.399	9.681	.000*
4.	Self Success	0.198	4.716	.000*

R Square = 0.421, Adjusted R square = 0.416, F–change = 22.239, Durbin Watson – 2.322
*Significant at 1%, **Significant at 5%

Table 3.3 reveals the results of regression analysis. Independent variables explained 42.1 per cent of variance of emotional intelligence (F change = 22.239, $p < .05$). The result indicates that there are three dimensions of personal competencies namely, people success ($\beta = 0.298, p < .01$), system success ($\beta = 0.399, p < .01$), and self success ($\beta = 0.198, p < .01$), which are positively associated with emotional intelligence. It can be therefore proposed that these three dimensions of personal competencies are directly responsible for presence and sustenance of emotional intelligence in Indian business organizations. Moreover it can be concluded from the findings that people success and system success of executives are the most important variables that explain the variance in emotional intelligence followed by self success. Thus hypothesis H1, H3 and H4 were confirmed.

However, one of the dimensions of personal competencies namely, task success ($\beta = 0.064, p > .05$) is not significantly related to emotional intelligence. Though it is one of the important competencies for the executive to possess but the contribution made by it to emotional intelligence is not direct. Thus hypothesis H2 is not confirmed as its significance level is > than .05.

DISCUSSION

Indian economy is moving towards high-tech: high-touch, service based stage of development, which presents new challenges for Human Resource Management. Competencies like managing one's emotions, handling conflicts, teamwork, leadership, motivation, interpersonal sensitivity, skills at negotiation and personal or internal qualities like empathy, initiative, adaptability, confidence and optimism are much more crucial than academic competence, technical expertise and professional education which constitute relatively only a small part of the picture. This transformation represents a shift from traditional intelligence or cognitive intelligence measured by Intelligence Quotient (IQ) to emotional Intelligence measured by Emotional Quotient (EQ). This study is designed to gain an insight into the development of emotional intelligence on the basis of personal competencies. It has been proposed in the study that it is essential for the executives of the present day business to possess high emotional intelligence and personal competencies impact the presence of emotional intelligence.

The results of the study indicate that people success is one of the important constructs of personal competencies and is strongly related to emotional intelligence. It therefore suggests that an understanding of the ability to relate well with each other in the organizational context paves the way for high emotional intelligence. This has been also supported by the study done by Singh (2007) where it was found that ability to form effective relationships at work place results in high efficiency of employees. Further Jordan and Troth (2004) also suggested that team performance was directly related to the emotional intelligence of employees in organizations.

The study also indicates the importance of system success in predicting emotional intelligence of executives in Indian Business organizations. The competency of system success fosters individuals to focus on the organizational issues and identify with the organizational variables that control his or her performance and satisfaction. This finding is supported with the study by Sy, Tram and O'Hara (2006) which reported a strong relationship between emotional intelligence and job performance and satisfaction. Rosete and Ciarrochi (2005) also suggest that a strong association between emotional intelligence and workplace effectiveness lead to system success. Further in a study on 100 bank employees by Manila University (cited in D. Singh 2001) it was found that IQ scores were virtually unrelated with job performance whereas, EQ had high association with job performance.

Besides this, self success, one of the dimensions of personal competencies also contributes to predict emotional intelligence. Self success is an indicator of self-awareness which helps a person to comprehend one's emotions and recognize its impact on their decisions. Stein and Book (2006) suggested that and emotionally intelligent person is able to identify ones own feelings and to know the cause behind them thereby leading to self success. Further a national survey of American employers revealed that six of seven desired traits for entry-level workers were non-academic (Goleman, 1998) and were related to the understanding and recognition of self and others feelings and taking appropriate actions (Sims, 1998)

However, task success was found to be a low predictor of emotional intelligence. This finding highlights that the ability of the individual to focus on the current task in hand and do it effectively does not have strong association with emotional intelligence. It could be more of a factor of cognitive intelligence rather than emotional intelligence. This finding can be supported by Goldman's (1995, 1998) argument that task performance may not be directly related to emotional intelligence except for providing a bedrock for other competencies to be successful. This has been further supported by (Cavallo & Brienza, 2002). However this finding is in contrast to the study by Jaeger (2003) which revealed a strong association between emotional intelligence and employee performance leading to task success. With respect to the model proposed the result of the present study can be depicted as follows:

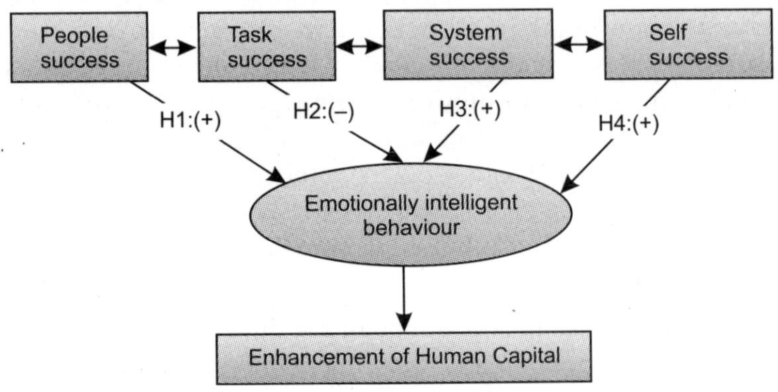

Fig. 3.2 : Results depicted in the proposed model

Overall the study provides enough evidence to prove that any improvement in the level of personal competencies of executives in the business organization is likely to improve the level of emotional intelligence of the employees too. Therefore to enhance the emotional intelligence of employees in organization, management has to aim to improve the levels of personal competencies of its employees. Employees in organization have to be trained for developing their people focus so that they can have better interpersonal relationship and connectivity in the organization. Management also has to dwell upon the focus on the way the organization operates its systems and processes and train its people to work effectively to work on the existing systems to add on to their levels of emotional intelligence. Besides this individuals have to be emphasized to have a focus on completion of their tasks and lead to its success along with the development of self. All these efforts on the part of the management will help in creating an organization which comprises of emotionally intelligent employees and add to the human capital of the organization.

CONCLUDING COMMENTS

The study reports an investigation of the relationship between the dimensions of personal competencies and emotional intelligence of executives working in Indian Business organizations. In the present study personal competencies were identified and studied as independent variables that influence the presence of emotional intelligence. To enhance the emotional intelligence of executives organizations have to enhance the competencies of people success, system success and self success.

Human Problems have three dimensions: material, social and metaphysical. Even after adoption of all the external or environmental focus approaches like job enrichment or enlargement, management by objectives, management by exception and participative management; every organization experiences behavioural problems like low level job involvement, job satisfaction and productivity on the one hand and high employee turnover and absenteeism, stress, communication gaps and lack of trust amongst employees on the other hand. The above-mentioned approaches might have failed because they consider the material and social dimensions of human resource only and not the emotional.

To grow and develop in the present kaleidoscopic scenario organizations need to constantly focus on learning so as to gain sustainable competitive advantage. This requires organizations to undertake continuous training and development efforts to impart cognitive as well as emotional learning. Most management and executive development efforts are targeted ton work on non-intellective and non-cognitive aspects or competencies such as self-management, motivation, teamwork, conflict management, stress management, leadership, empathy, sales and customer relations etc.; so that the individual and organizational goals can be attained by engaging organizational members in the desired patterns of thought, feeling and action. Irrespective of the national boundaries, the outcome of this study can be universally employed to the employees of any organization for the purpose of improving their emotional intelligence so that their competence and effectiveness at the job gets enhanced.

The above mentioned findings can lead us to conclude that emotional intelligence is one of the prerequisite for the success of any business enterprise. Emotional intelligence is an ability which can be developed among people with exposure and training. The existence of personal competencies among people has a major role to play in developing and enhancing the emotional intelligence of employees in business organizations. An attempt to develop the personal competencies of executives in organization can go a long way to improve their emotional intelligence. These efforts are to be made from both the sides *i.e.,* the management and the employees to create a culture in the organization in which competencies are enhanced through training and development which then add up to level of emotional intelligence of the working executives.

A major step in this direction can be the played by the leaders who have to keep their employees in high self esteem and create an environment where there is openness in sharing of ideas and thoughts. Employees have to be encouraged to develop their social skills which would lead to their greater acceptance among their colleagues and subordinates thereby smoothening the work process leading to success in the organization. There may be a discontentment that personal growth in the organizations is not encouraged and rewarded though there are lots of possibilities to be experimental and inventive. Management has to encourage people to experiment with the systems and processes leading to personal and organizational growth.

Scope for Further Research

The present study leaves a lot of scope for further research in the area of Emotional Intelligence and Personal competencies. Some of the specific ones are:

1. The researcher in future can do a comparative analysis to find the difference between private and public sector

organizations in relation to their levels of emotional intelligence and personal competencies.

2. An international comparison between developed and developing economies will help us become aware of the major transitions taking place in the area of emotional intelligence at the global level.
3. An extensive study of formal implementation of the developmental programs to enhance the emotional intelligence of executives in business organizations could be carried out to facilitate effective and congenial work environment.

REFERENCES

1. Boyatzis, R. (1982). The *Competent Manager: A Model for Effective Performance*. New York: John Wiley and Sons.
2. Bunker, K.A. (1997). The Power of Vulnerability in Contemporary Leadership, *Consulting Psychology Journal*, 49 (2), 122-136.
3. Campbell, D.P. (1990). *Inklings, Issues and Observations*, 10, 11-12.
4. Cavallo, K., Brienza, D. (2002), "Emotional Competence and Leadership Excellence at Johnson and Johnson, *The Emotional Intelligence and Leadership Study*", available at: www.corpconsultinggroup.com,
5. Cherniss, C. (2001). Emotional Intelligence and Organizational Effectiveness. In C. Cherniss & D. Goleman (Eds.). *The Emotionally Intelligent Workplace* (pp. 3-26). San Francisco: Jossey-Bass.
6. Crawford, L. (1997). A Global Approach to Project Management Competence. *Paper presented to Proceedings of the 1997 AIPM National Conference*, Gold Coast.
7. Elankumaran, S., Rekha, S. & Anwar, H. (2005). Transcending Transformation: Enlightening Endeavours at Tata Steel, *Journal of Business Ethics*, 59:109-119.
8. Finn, R. (1993), "A Synthesis of Current Research on Management Competencies", *Working Paper No. 10-93*, Henley College, Henley-on-Thames.
9. Goleman, D. (1995). *Emotional Intelligence*. New York: Bantam.

10. Goleman, D. (1998). *Working with Emotional Intelligence*. New York: Bantam Books.
11. Gonczi, A. and Hagar, P. (1992). *Research Paper No 7L*. Heywood, A Guide to the Development of Competency Based Standards for Professions, National Office of Overseas Skills Recognition, Canberra.
12. Gonczi, A., Hagar, P. and Oliver, L (1990). *Research Paper No 1A*., Establishing Competency Based Standards in the Professions, Australian Government Publishing Service, Canberra.
13. Hunter, J. B. & Hunter, R. F. (1984). Validity and Utility of Alternative Predictors of Job Performance. *Psychological Bulletin*, 96, 72-98.
14. Jaeger, A.J. (2003). Job Competencies and the Curriculum: An Inquiry into Emotional Intelligence in Graduate Professional Education. *Research in Higher Education*, 44(6), 615-639.
15. Jordan, P. J. & Troth, A. C. (2004). Managing Emotions During Team Problem Solving: Emotional intelligence and Conflict Resolution. *Human Performance*, 17(2), 195-218.
16. Lopes, P. N., Grewal, D., Kadis, J., Gall, M., & Salovey, P. (2006). Evidence that Emotional Intelligence is Related to Job Performance and Affect and Attitudes at Work. *Psicothema*, 18, 132-138.
17. Lyons, J. B. & Schneider, T. R. (2005). The Influence of Emotional Intelligence on Performance. *Personality and Individual Differences*, 39(4), 693-703.
18. Mayer, J. D., Salovey, P., & Caruso, D. R. (2000). Emotional Intelligence as Zeitgeist, as Personality, and as a Mental Ability. In R. Bar-On and J.D.A. Parker (Eds.), *Handbook of Emotional Intelligence* (pp. 92-117). San Francisco: Jossey-Bass.
19. Orme, G. & Langhorn, S. (2003). Lessons Learned from Implementing EI Programme—The Cutting Edge of Emotional Intelligence Programs. Competency and Emotional Intelligence Quarterly: *The Journal of Performance through People*, Vol. 10, No. 2, Winter, pp. 32-39
20. Parry, S.B. (1998), "Just What is a Competency? (And Why Should You Care?)", *Training*, Vol. 35, No. 6, pp. 58-64.
21. Punia, B.K. (2004). Emotional Intelligence and Leadership Behaviour of Indian Executives—An Exploratory Study. *Unpublished Ph.D. Thesis*.
22. Rosete, D. & Ciarrochi, J. (2005). Emotional Intelligence and Its Relationship to Workplace Performance. *Leadership and Organization Development Journal*, 26(5), 388-399.

23. Ryback, D. (1998). *Putting Emotional Intelligence to Work: Successful Leadership is More Than Just IQ*, Boston, MA: Butterworth-Heinemann.

24. Salovey, P. & Mayer, J.D. (1990). *Emotional Intelligence. Imagination, Cognition and Personality*, 9, 185-221.

25. Schmidt, F. L. & Hunter, J. B. (1981). Employment Testing: Old Theories and New Research Findings. *American Psychologist* , 36, 1128-1137.

26. Sims, B. (1998, November 8). Handling Emotions While on the Job. *The Eagle*, p. E2.

27. Singh, D. (2001). *Emotional Intelligence at Work: A Professional Guide*, New Delhi: Sage.

28. Singh, K. (2005). *Organization Change and Development*. Excel Books, New Delhi.

29. Singh, S. K. (2007). Emotional Intelligence and Organisational Leadership: A Gender Study in Indian Context. *International Journal of Indian Culture and Business Management*, 1 (1/2), 48-63.

30. Spencer, L. M. and Spencer, S. M. (1993). *Competence at Work*. NY: Wiley.

31. Stein, S.J. & H.E. Book (2006). EQ Edge: *Emotional Intelligence and Your Success*. Wiley, John & Sons, Incorporated.

32. Sternberg, R. J. (1997). *Successful Intelligence*. New York: Plume. Sy, T., Tram, S., & O'Hara, L. (2006). Relation of Employee and Manager emotional Intelligence to Job Satisfaction and Performance. *Journal of Vocational Behaviour*, 68(3), 461-473.

33. Zipkin, A. (2000, May 31). *The Wisdom of Thoughtfulness*. New York Times, pp. C1-C10.

CHAPTER

Effectiveness of a Conflict Resolution Training Programme

Changing Graduate Students Style of Managing Conflict with Their Faculty Advisors

ABSTRACT

We investigated the conflict management preferences of graduate students with their faculty advisors and assessed the effects of participating in a conflict resolution workshop on those preferences. One hundred and twenty-one graduate students completed the pre-workshop surveys, and 69 participants completed the post-workshop surveys after seven workshops conducted over a 3 year period. Nineteen subjects participated in three post-workshop focus groups. The quantitative pre-workshop data showed that avoidance and accommodation styles for managing conflict were preferred among participants. Participants showed a trend towards a statistically significant increase in the collaborating score post-workshop relative to pre-workshop levels. The qualitative data indicated that students applied skills taught during the workshop, including interest-based principles, when interacting with faculty.

Key words : *conflict resolution. Graduate education, Negotiation*

Graduate students, especially those at the doctoral level, regard their relationships with faculty members as a critically important determinant of the quality of their graduate experience (Adrian-Taylor *et al.,* 2007; Green and Bauer 1995; Harnett and Katz 1977; Nerad and Miller 1996; Wade-Benzoni *et al.,* 2006). Conflict between graduate students and faculty advisors can impair the graduate student-faculty relationship, with negative consequences for both parties (Adrian-Taylor *et al.,* 2007; Golde 2000; Keltner 1998; Lovitts 2001; Nerad and Miller 1996), but especially for the graduate student. For example, the destructive consequences of interpersonal conflict for graduate students and their faculty advisors may include internal loss such as self-worth, control, or confidence, as well as external loss such as funding, mentoring support, research opportunities, or even a missed career due to not completing the degree program. Conversely, constructive consequences may lead to a variety of personal and professional gains for both the graduate student and faculty advisor. Therefore, efforts to maintain and foster the graduate student-faculty advisor relationship by preventing and constructively managing conflict are important.

One salient feature of the student-advisor relationship is the power differential that exists between the two individuals. This power differential often determines the way graduate students and faculty members manage conflicts, but individual preferences or conflict management styles are also important determinants of how effectively conflicts are resolved (Rubin *et al.,* 1994). Ultimately, the combination of how both parties manage conflict within a particular context determines whether the outcome is desirable or undesirable. We next discuss the themes of power and conflict management style and how they impact the relationships between graduate students and faculty advisors as they face conflicts associated with graduate education.

The Graduate Student/Faculty Advisor Relationship A power differential, whether perceived or actual, exists within the graduate student/faculty advisor relationship. Damrosch (1995) referred to the faculty advisor as a 'paternal authority', paralleling the traditional

German term for the dissertation faculty advisor: the Doktorvater or Doctor Father. The paternalistic image of the Doktorvater leads graduate students to perceive the faculty as extremely powerful. This perception, coupled with the organizational expectation that faculty members function as the "gatekeepers" of the disciplines, creates a power gap, which graduate students see as insurmountable. Graduate education can also be likened to an apprenticeship model (Baird 1995), where the younger workers must please their 'masters' with their handiwork, knowing that the work is not 'right' until the 'master' deems it so. Graduate student perceptions of their faculty advisors' power are related to a number of variables critical to student satisfaction and success. (Aquinis *et al.,* 1996).

Due to the power differential, which characterizes many graduate student/faculty relationships, graduate students often feel helpless when conflict arises between themselves and their faculty advisors. Furthermore, they are largely unaware that options other than confrontation, avoidance, or accommodation exist. That graduate students so often turn to Innov High Educ passive strategies when facing conflicts (*i.e.,* avoidance or accommodation) may explain why some faculty advisors do not recognize or accept the existence of conflict. Holton (1998) captured the nature of the problem when she stated that, "For years, we in higher education were able to hide—or at least vociferously deny—the existence of conflict... much conflict in higher education was managed by avoidance." (p.xiii). In fact, one of the authors of this article recalls a conversation she had with an associate dean of a graduate school who reported that conflict between graduate students and faculty 'did not exist' on his campus. In their book about management skills for scientists, Cohen and Cohen (2005) made similar observations about laboratory scientists' 'aversion to admitting that a problem exists' (p. 57), in part because they do not know how to manage those situations.

Lovitts (2004) suggested that departments work more closely with faculty advisors to "establish mentoring and interaction styles that lead to higher levels of student satisfaction." (p.135). Austin

(2002) specifically recommended that deans and chairs work with the faculty to develop effective advising relationships, including ways to manage conflict if it occurs. In response to these recommendations from the literature, in 1997 the Graduate School of Michigan State University developed a six-hour workshop, which is offered to graduate students and faculty members and focuses on the importance of the graduate student-faculty advisor relationship for both parties and on how various approaches to managing conflict can impact that relationship (Klomparens *et al.* 2008). The personal preferences of graduate students when managing conflicts with faculty members and how these preferences might change as a result of participating in this conflict management workshop (Klomparens *et al.,* 2008) were the focus of our study.

Background

Particular conflict management strategies have their advantages and disadvantages and are more or less effective depending on the type of conflict and the situation or context in which the conflict occurs (Lewicki *et al.,* 2003; Sandy *et al.,* 2006). The Dual Concern Model (Rubin *et al.,* 1994), based on the work of Blake and Mouton (1964), is the most widely used approach to describe styles or strategies used to manage conflict. It provides the theoretical foundation for the instruments we used in this study. Among the five styles of the Dual Concern Model, the collaborative style is the one which creates an environment where relationships are preserved and sometimes fostered. Because the relationships between graduate students and their faculty advisors are so critical, the workshop that we evaluated in our study promotes using a collaborative style referred to as the interest-based approach. The interest-based approach (Fisher and Ury, 1991) is a process of resolving conflict that seeks to satisfy the interests of the parties involved in a conflict.

The Workshop

The workshop that is the focus of this study is described in detail in Klomparens *et al.,* (2008). It is entitled "Setting Expectations and

Resolving Conflict between Graduate Students and Faculty" and is sponsored by the Graduate School at Michigan State University. One of the features of the workshop is the examination of the strengths and weaknesses of several options for managing conflict between graduate students and faculty. First, it addresses how avoiding managing a conflict is rarely an optimal strategy in graduate education since the number of options to resolve an issue often diminish over time. Accommodation is presented as a strategy, but its limitations are explained making reference to feelings of resentment that accumulate over time. The workshop then focuses on the negative professional consequences likely to arise from a competitive approach, which can damage the faculty-student relationship. Most importantly, the presenters explain how an interest-based approach serves to deal with conflict in a cooperative mode, which protects and strengthens the relationship between graduate students and key faculty members, particularly their major professors. Thus, while different approaches for managing conflict are discussed in the workshop, an interest-based, collaborative strategy is strongly endorsed; and the participants practice the implementation of that approach in a variety of situations germane to graduate education (Klomparens *et al.,* 2008).

In addition to principles of interest-based negotiation, the workshop presenters teach communication skills and strategies to foster effective interactions with faculty members, including how to prepare for meetings with advisors and committee members. Participants are encouraged to use interest-based principles, not only when managing conflicts, but also when they jointly set expectations with faculty (for a full description of the workshop, visit http://grad.msu.edu/conflictresolution/).

Conflict Style Assessment

There are several instruments available to assess individual conflict managing styles. Among the most popular are those developed by Blake and Mouton (1964), Hall (1969), Thomas and Kilmann (1974), Putnam and Wilson (1982), and Rahim (1983). Adult educators often use these tools to evaluate the impact of conflict resolution training interventions by comparing conflict resolution styles before and after an intervention (Deen 2000; Johnson 1992; Mikheev 2006; Rashid 2001; Watt 1994). Findings from these studies are mixed. For example, Mikheev (2006) used an experimental design to evaluate the efficacy of a conflict resolution curriculum in reducing peer victimization and increasing the use of a cooperative strategy. The self-reported data suggested that the intervention significantly increased the treatment group's use of a cooperative strategy in resolving conflict, while decreasing the use of avoidance in conflict situations. In contrast, Deen (2000) found no difference in the conflict resolution styles of 4-H leader volunteers who had participated in conflict resolution training and those who had not participated in the training.

An evaluation of the impact of different interventions on conflict resolution styles has never been implemented with a sample of graduate students, as recommended by Rashid (2001). Furthermore, though the efficacy of conflict resolution training has been assessed in ways other than through use of the popular instruments described above (Zweibel *et al.,* 2008), we know of no study which has combined quantitative and qualitative approaches to examine the impact of participating in a conflict resolution workshop. Using such a mixedmethods approach has several advantages (Creswell 1994), including triangulation of data sources, surfacing of similar and contradictory findings, and the expansion of the breadth and scope of information. In our study we used that approach to determine if participating in a conflict resolution training programme results in a change in self-reported conflict managing style and in the adoption of skills and strategies endorsed in that workshop.

The Study

In the workshop the facilitators devote a significant amount of time to the discussion of competitive strategies because anecdotal data from those who advise graduate students in conflict situations (*e.g.* the University Ombudsman, senior staff of the Graduate School) suggest that often that is the style they adopt when confronting conflicts with faculty members. These anecdotal observations, which the Michigan State University Graduate School has collected over several years, clash with the results of studies in which avoidance and accommodation, rather than competition, are identified as the most common strategies used by students facing conflicts with faculty members (Adrian-Taylor *et al.*, 2007; Zweibel *et al.,* 2008). Thus, one specific aim of this study was to use pre-workshop quantitative data to determine the initial style of conflict management preferred by the participants. We wanted to determine if participation in a six-hour conflict resolution workshop, using an interactive teaching method, would enhance the students' understanding of the interest based approach to resolving conflict and change their self-reported style of conflict management. The effectiveness of the workshop would be supported if the participant's scores showed a significant change in conflict resolution style from pre- to post-workshop, such that the post-workshop scores are higher for collaboration, which is the strategy endorsed by the workshop. This represents an 'alpha change', which is based on a comparison of self-reports before and after a particular intervention, as described by Golembiewski *et al.,* (1976). In addition, qualitative data were used to determine if the participants had adopted the communication skills and strategies endorsed by the workshop when interacting with their faculty advisors.

Method

This study was conducted over a 3 year period. One hundred and twenty-one graduate students completed the pre-workshop surveys prior to the start of each of seven workshops, and 69 participants completed the post-workshop surveys. Nineteen self-selected subjects participated in one of three focus group sessions approximately 5 months following their participation in the workshop. Analysis of the transcripts of the focus groups was used to determine if the participants had engaged in the use of the interest-based approach to resolve conflicts with their faculty advisors following the workshop. Finally, an additional 65 graduate students received the pre-workshop survey. Different from the study sample, these 65 students did not voluntarily enroll in the target workshop; rather they were participants in a University required three-day workshop and orientation for teaching assistants. We then used these data to test the generality of the pre-workshop profile obtained for the study sample.

Participants

Participants were graduate students who voluntarily enrolled in the "Setting Expectations and Resolving Conflict between Graduate Students and Faculty" workshop. Table 4.1 summarizes the demographic data for the study sample as well as for the teaching assistants who only completed the pre-survey. Of the 120 participants 50 per cent were international graduate students, and 50 per cent were domestic graduate students. The domestic students consisted of 76 per cent Caucasian; 10 per cent African–American; and the remaining 5 per cent comprised of Mexican-American, Hispanic, or Asian/Pacific Islanders. Most students (57%) indicated that they had recently begun their coursework.

Table 4.1 Demographics for study sample (SS) and graduate teaching assistants (GTA)

	Gender	Age	Programme	Domestic/ International
SS	42 male 78 female	35% (18-25 years old) 40% (26-35 years old) 15% (36-45 years old) 10% (46 or older)	50% doctoral 48% masters	50% domestic 50% int'l
GTA	33 male 32 female	60% (18-25 years old) 37% (26-35 years old) 3% (36-45 years old)	65% doctoral 35% masters	62% domestic 38% int'l

Not all students provided complete demographic information even though they responded to the survey questions. Approximately 9 per cent of the students did not report their ethnicity, and 2 per cent did not indicate whether they were doctoral or master level students of the 65 students who participated in the required teaching assistant training program 38 per cent were international students, and 62 per cent were domestic. The domestic students consisted of 77 per cent Caucasian, 10 per cent African American, 5 per cent Asian–American; and 4 per cent were Mexican-American, Hispanic, or Native American students.

Procedures

Graduate secretaries sent an email announcement of the workshop to all graduate students, and fliers were posted on campus. Each workshop accommodated approximately 30 participants. The announced focus of the workshop was to teach communication skills and collaborative approaches for 'preventing and resolving conflict' in the relationships between faculty members and graduate students.

At the start of the workshop, a researcher who was not a workshop facilitator introduced the evaluation procedure. Participants were presented with an institutionally approved consent form that provided information about confidentiality, voluntary participation and their rights as research subjects, the pre-workshop survey instrument, and contact information form. After the participants completed the consent form and the survey, the researcher gathered the materials and exited the location. The 6-hour workshop was conducted by three faculty members from the Graduate School. Ten weeks later, a post-survey instrument was mailed to the participants, with a self-addressed, stamped return envelope. Subsequently, we sent two reminders to those who did not return the survey immediately, resulting in a total post-intervention participation rate of 57 per cent.

Approximately 5 months following each workshop, subjects were invited to participate in a focus group. A financial incentive of $20.00 and lunch was offered to those who did so. Focus group interviews were semi-structured and lasted approximately 1.5 hours. Interview sessions were tape recorded and transcribed.

Measures

The Thomas-Kilmann Conflict Mode Instrument (TKI) (Thomas and Kilmann 1974) and the Organizational Communication Conflict Instrument (OCCI) (Putnam and Wilson 1982) were chosen as the pre-post survey measures of conflict style and behaviour. The TKI is the most widely used and one of the best known instruments (Van de Vliert and Kabanoff 1990) in both research and training due to its ease of administration and value in uncovering individual style differences (Womack 1988). Coupled with the OCCI, the pre and post-test we administered to participants provided for a combined fixed choice and Likert scale response strategy. In addition, the OCCI lent itself well to the addition of a contextual situation in which participants could identify their behavioural responses. Further, the specific wording of both instruments was common enough that international student, whose second language was English, would understand the choices they were making. Because of these positive features, these instruments were selected over others of somewhat higher validity (Van de Vliert 1997). Thomas-Kilmann Conflict Mode Instrument (TKI) (Thomas and Kilmann 1974). This measure assesses typical response styles to conflict situations. An adapted version of the original 30-item measure that assesses five modes of conflict-handling skills—competing, collaborating, compromising, avoiding, and accommodating—was used. It is a forced choice questionnaire, in which respondents choose between two statements per item, each of which reflects the likelihood for one of the response styles; scores are summed across each response style. For this study, items were split into two parallel forms. Since each of the subscales had an odd number of items, one item was excluded based on face validity from each of these subscales in order to have an equal number of items within each subscale at each assessment. This resulted in 10 items on the pre-test and 10 items on the post-test surveys.

The five modes of conflict management skills are conceptualized within a two-dimensional model along assertiveness and cooperativeness. The internal consistency coefficients for this instrument are in the moderate range. Organizational Communication Conflict Instrument (OCCI) (Putnam and Wilson 1982). Conflict resolution style was assessed using an adapted version of the original 30-item measure, which assesses communicative behaviors in the management of interpersonal conflict. The scale derives three scores each for non-confrontation, solution-orientation, and control. Of these, solution-orientation is considered to represent a more desirable conflict resolution style. These factors instantiate the five conflict orientations of competing, collaborating, compromising, avoiding, and accommodating (Thomas and Kilmann 1974), such that avoiding and accommodating on the TKI represent non-confrontation, compromising and collaborating on the TKI both represent solution orientation, and competing on the TKI represents control. Each of the three subscales describes concrete verbal and/or non-verbal behaviours and focuses on goal-oriented disagreements. For this study, items were split into two parallel forms. Fourteen items from each instrument were combined to construct the pre-test survey, and fourteen items from each instrument were combined to construct the post-test survey. The two subscales of solution orientation and control had an odd number of items.

Hence, one item was excluded from each of these subscales in order to have an equal number of items within each subscale. Participants were asked by the evaluator to consider past disagreements with supervisors and then asked to rate how often they were likely to respond as described in a statement on a 7-point Likert scale ranging from 1 (always) to 7 (never). Example items include 'I assert my opinion forcefully' and 'I steer clear of disagreeable situations.' Putnam and Wilson (1982) reported subscale coefficient alphas of 0.88 for non-confrontation, 0.83 for solution orientation, and 0.77 for control. Focus Groups To reduce the influence of social desirability demands (*e.g.,* the tendency to comply with social demands) (Crowne and Marlowe 1964) on the comments of the focus group participants, the semi-structured focus groups were facilitated by an Outreach Specialist from a department unrelated to the Graduate School. This Outreach Specialist does not teach or mentor graduate students as a part of her regular duties, was not involved in the presentation of the workshop or in the overall evaluation study, and is an expert in qualitative methodology. The facilitator moderated the sessions guided by a protocol with the following questions. Do graduate students attempt to prevent or manage conflict with faculty? Can you describe a conflict you experienced with your faculty advisor(s)? How did you manage that conflict? Can you describe any barriers you encountered to managing conflict with your advisor(s)? What advice would you give to new graduate students about how to manage conflict with their advisor(s)? The protocol allowed the facilitator to ask clarifying questions in response to participants' answers to the main protocol questions.

Content analysis was used to evaluate the focus group transcripts. Content analysis is the "process of identifying, coding and categorizing the primary patterns in the data" (Patton 1990). Triangulation (Patton 1990) was achieved by using multiple analysts and conducting three focus group sessions approximately 5 months following participation in a workshop. Four researchers knowledgeable about interest-based principles, as well as content analysis of transcripts, independently analyzed the transcripts. For the analysis, researchers first read two of the three transcripts several times, highlighting statements related to conflict resolution and student-faculty interactions and aspects of their relationships. Second, the four researchers met to discuss their preliminary interpretations of the interviews and to reach agreement on the major themes and patterns. These themes and patterns were then used deductively while reading the third interview protocol. Following this review, the researchers once again met to discuss how well the themes and patterns in the first and second transcripts compared with the data in the third transcript, highlighting any additional themes. Finally, a master list of nine categories was generated and read comparatively against each transcript. A consensus among the researchers was reached in support of the final categories as a reflection of all transcripts analyzed. In the final stageof analysis, themes from the transcripts were compared with the results from the quantitative analysis to identify common patterns, as well as possible contradictions between the two data sets.

RESULTS

Quantitative

We conducted paired samples t-tests with each of the TKI and OCCI subscales as outcomes to compare pre-and post responses. Because the approach involved multiple comparisons, the Bonferroni method (Bryman and Cramer 2005) was used to adjust the significance levels. This method divides the conventional level of significance (0.05) by the number of comparisons, thus resulting in significance levels of 0.01 for the TKI and 0.02 for the OCCI. We conducted all analyses using the Statistical Package for Social Sciences version 16.0. Analysis exclusion was utilized for individuals missing post workshop data.

For the TKI, results from the paired t-tests indicated that participants showed a trend towards a statistically significant increase in collaborating behaviors post-workshop relative to the pre-workshop levels [$t(64) = -2.14, p < .04$]. This was accompanied by an apparent reduction in the competing subscale score (Fig. 4.1), but that change was also not statistically significant [$t(64) = 1.14$, ns]. There were no significant differences on the avoiding [$t(64) = 1.11$, ns],compromising [$t(64) = -0.50$, ns], and accommodating [$t(64) = 0.07$, ns] subscales post-workshop relative to pre-workshop levels (*See Fig. 4.1 on next page*). In general, competing was the least used response style, while compromising, avoiding, and accommodating were the most frequent response styles in conflict situations. These preferences for response styles were consistent across pre-and post-workshop assessments. Similar preferences in response styles were also noted in the sample of 65 graduate students recruited from teaching assistantship workshops (*See Fig. 4.2 on page 66*). For both the study sample and the graduate teaching assistant group, no significant differences were found between domestic and international students on any of the quantitative measures.

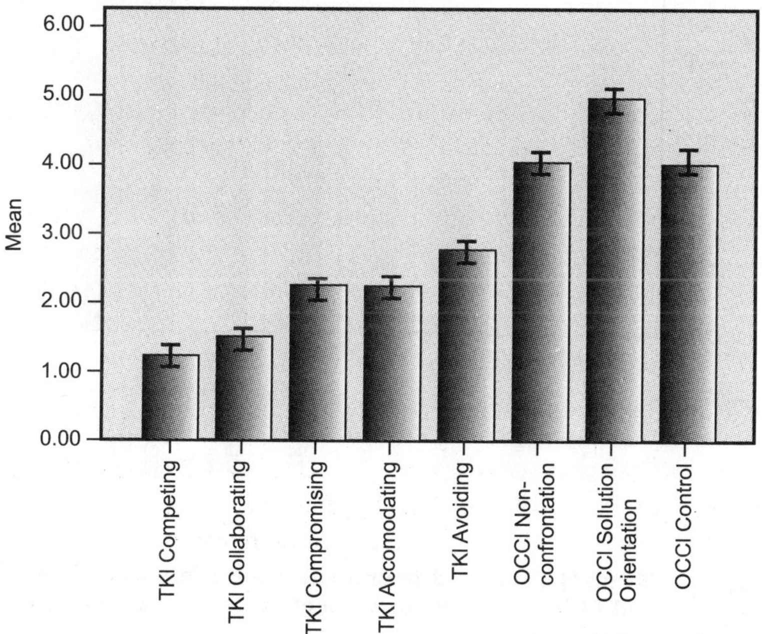

Fig. 4.1 Means (± 1 Standard Error of the Mean) of pre-workshop TKI and OCCI outcomes for students recruited from teaching workshops.

The 3 subscales of the OCCI, non-confrontation, solution-orientation, and control, were examined as outcomes. There were no significant mean differences on the nonconfrontation [*t*(68) = 0.72, ns], solution orientation [*t*(68) = "0.20, ns], or controlling [*t* (68) = 0.80, ns] subscales post-workshop, relative to pre-workshop levels (*See Fig. 4.3 on page 68*). Qualitative.

The analysis of the focus group transcripts revealed several main themes. First, graduate students described the relationship with their faculty advisor(s) as playing a critical role in their graduate program experience. Second, graduate students perceived a power

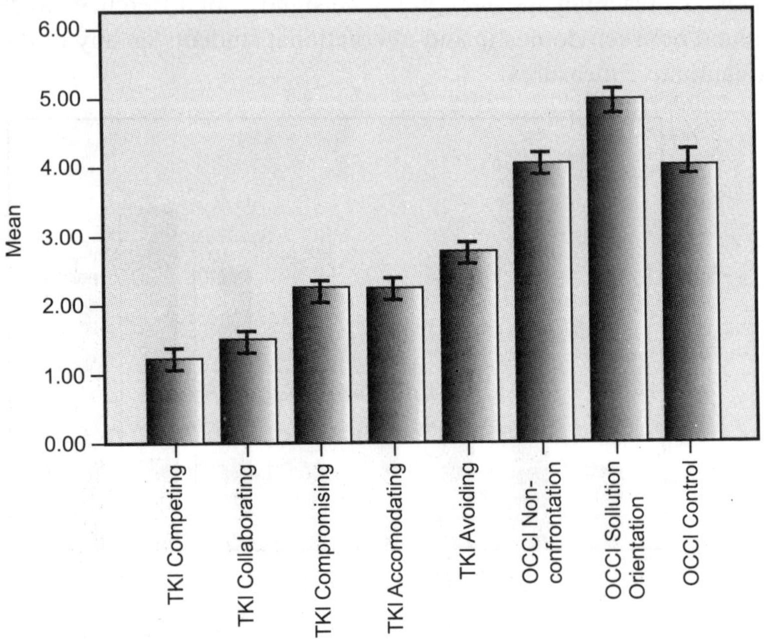

Fig. 4.2 Means (± 1 Standard Error of the Mean) of pre-workshop TKI and OCCI outcomes for students recruited from teaching workshops.

differential between themselves and their faculty advisor(s). Third, strategies of avoidance and accommodation were the preferred ways to prevent or manage conflict. Fourth, support from others, who are independent of their faculty advisor(s), aided them in managing conflict; and fifth, graduate students expressed differing insights from the training experience, which was reflected in their practicing various elements of the interest-based approach and in their adoption of communication strategies taught in the workshop.

The Faculty/Student Relationship The faculty/student relationship was discussed at length throughout the focus group sessions. The relationship was portrayed in terms of its power differential and the ways in which graduate students shape their own behavior to ensure a positive experience. As one participant stated, "The primary thing is that we all look for good relationships with our advisors." The awareness of a power differential was expressed in different ways, from the faculty member being referred to as 'the boss' and 'you're depending on that person' to the faculty advisor being labelled 'a slave-driver'.

Participants talked openly about the ways in which they 'ensure' a positive experience with their advisors by carefully monitoring their own behavior. One participant mentioned that she 'stifles' herself and must be 'very, very careful' even though she believes she has an open relationship with her advisor. Another stated, 'My professor's opinion of my abilities is my number one concern... I'm always trying to avoid saying something that will sort of reveal my innermost dumbness." Others simply wait for the passage of time, "So I'm pretty much just waiting for things to naturally get more familiar and for the relationship to kind of strengthen on time alone because I don't have too many things that I'm spinning out."

Discussion regarding the faculty/student relationship was generally coupled with comments reflecting empathy for faculty advisors. Though some participants felt that the lack of time spent with their faculty advisor was hindering their progress toward the degree, many also felt that faculty advisors were doing the best they could with the time they had. As one participant stated, "...all of our advisors are so busy, and they have so many things that they need to be doing, it's really hard for them to commit the time to take a significant interest in what we're doing...." In fact, some participants shared their thoughts about their advisor's multiple responsibilities as well as their 'humanness'. This is illustrated in the following comments, "...he has so many other things on his plate...he is not just in charge of students, he has other faculty that he has to work with on either funding or this or that. He's got four or five post-docs as well. So it is a big group." In terms of their 'humanness', one participant stated, "...look at the professor just as a human being. Everyone has good things and also bad things. The professor might be high I.Q., maybe get high authority. But he

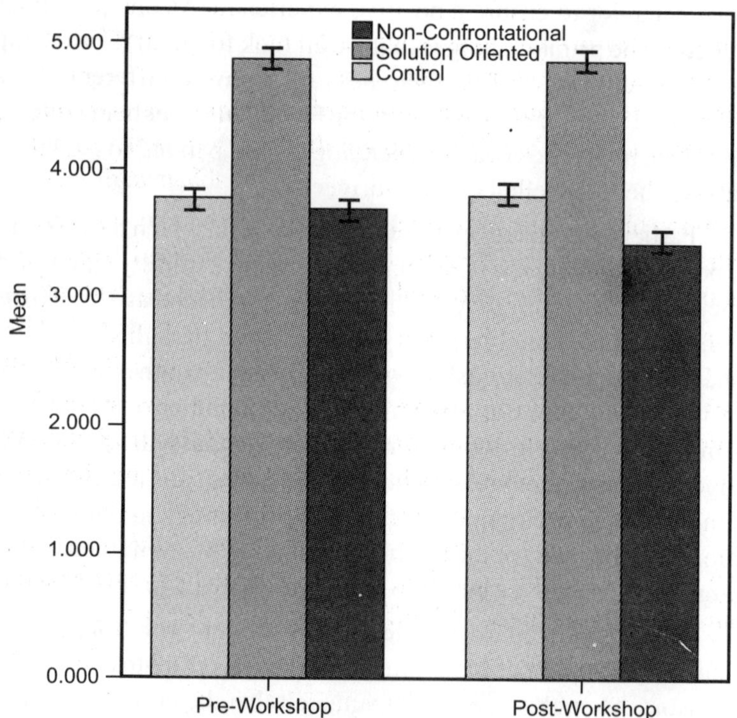

Fig. 4.3 Means (± 1 Standard Error of the Mean) of OCCI outcomes pre and post-workshop

is or she is just a person, you know. He has feelings." Another stated, "But like, as I keep going, I realized that she's human. My advisor makes a ton of mistakes. You know, she's pretty new to the department, and so she's had me take classes that didn't count for anything." Avoidance The strategies for preventing and managing conflict with faculty mentioned consistently throughout the interviews were those of avoidance and accommodation. As one participant stated, "So those are my choices: ignore, argue (very rarely), or just do it, and accept it, and respect it, and just be glad that somebody's doing something." Participants spoke of avoidance as a way to prevent a conflict from occurring and as a Non-Confrontational Solution Oriented Control Pre-Workshop Post-

Workshop. Fig. 4.3 Means (± 1 Standard Error of the Mean) of OCCI outcomes pre- and post-workshop way to manage a conflict once it occurred. As a way to prevent conflict, one participant stated, "being careful of what you say on certain topics (that) you know could have bad consequences so you wisely avoid them…". In response to the question from the facilitator, "But it sounds as though you recognize the potential for conflict there and you are attempting to manage it?" another participant responded, "Yeah, by avoiding it."

Interestingly, participants expressed avoidance as a planned, proactive strategy as opposed to a reactive strategy. For example, one participant mentioned, "…being intelligent people, you can always find some way to avoid this complex situation (a conflict)." Another stated, "You always have (interests/hobbies) to fall back on when you have a conflict. So things are getting a little hot in the room. You just talk about the other thing."

To the researchers, this intentionality seemed at times to be extremely instrumental or utilitarian. For example, one student who works in a lab avoided a "time on task" conflict with her advisor by rearranging her hours, She (the advisor) doesn't really stick to the schedule that we came up with, and so we find ourselves starting to hold off coming into the office until noon, because we know if we come in at 8 am, she will have us working until 5. And so, if we come in at noon, and she only has us until 5, then we are closer to our 20 hours a week.

Similarly, some participants used their work habits to intentionally ward off potential conflict. Two participants in two separate focus group sessions illustrated this point: one stated, "I have no conflicts, I just work," and the other commented, "So my way of dealing with it is to simply just work, and just do my work, to work on my own."

Accommodating Participants spoke of accommodation as a way to prevent a conflict from occurring and to manage a conflict if it did occur. One participant stated, "I actually got to the give-up phase to where I was like I don't care, just tell me something to work on." Though participants did not reveal the nature of the phases that occurred prior to the 'give-up phase', accommodation was the path of least resistance. This all too common struggle can arise out of the power differential between the faculty advisor and their graduate student. As one participant described, "If you think you are inferior to your professor, you are going to say whatever he says and not really fight for what you want...". Another commented, "Somewhere along the line I just decided that he's probabiy right, so I'm just not going to argue with him, unless it's completely, really important to me, and then he'll listen. But I think that took a little bit of time to start to understand that."

Support from Others When asked about the strategies they use, participants offered insight into a preventative action that is commonly taken: support from others.I think one of the things that we've all been talking about this entire time is not to depend just on one person. Like don't get your advisor, and like cling to every word that they say, and take it as the be-all and end-all, like this is the fact. Talk to other people in the department, the faculty members, the administrative assistants. Know absolutely everything that there is to know. Or other graduate students, you know, probably have advice. So, just talking with, getting a broad base of support would be pretty helpful.

Other comments emphasized the importance of support. One commented, "...see what the other people think and get as many opinions as possible...because one person might not come up with the best idea, but more people's opinions will give you a better resolution." Another stated,

I found that I couldn't get what I want, at all. So I decided to reach other sources as much as possible. For example, the people and the faculty members in my school, other than the committee members I asked to read our papers. Or you know, if I have one very supportive committee member outside of school, so I get some advice from her.

Practicing Pieces Focus group participants reported that they had practiced various elements of the interest-based approach. The main theme that arose from these comments focused on the importance of preparing to meet with the faculty advisor. As one participant stated, "I remember from our previous workshop [that I should] come up with something organized and trying to bring a battle plan, not just show up and say, hey, what is this? Let's do something." Another participant stated, …pre-loading some thought into it I think has made all of our interaction more productive rather than just to show up. That was something I think I got out of it, just kind of much more defined plan is going to make all of these interactions with the professors more successful.

In addition to preparation, participants learned the importance of using time with their advisors wisely, in that, "The most important thing that I found is not only come prepared but also try to organize that time with that professor."

Reflection Overall, participants were highly satisfied with the workshop experience as illustrated by the following comments:

1. I did this at the end, and I think it would have been a million, million times more helpful if I would have sort of been able to do that earlier. But I think it is also a confidence builder, too. You have to get the confidence to sort of state your agenda. The thing that I actually learned a little bit from the conflict resolution is to not only just tell them what you want. Sort of make it a relationship. Show the advisor that this is in their best interest as well.
2. There is no doubt it was valuable. Maybe not for the specific topics of conflict resolution, but the stories and the things that I have heard have taught me a lot just about what to expect. And that's exactly what I wanted to get out of this. So that was good.
3. …that particular talk made it the most valuable workshop that I have had since I have been here. I think that should

be mandatory. But I always recommend it to people. But I seriously think that should be mandatory.

Discussion

One assumption that guided the initial development of the conflict resolution workshop assessed in our study was that competition is the preferred style for conflict management by graduate students. This assumption was based on reports by conflict mediators who are consulted by students when having problems with their graduate advisors. The data from both sets of quantitative data clearly failed to support that assumption. The Control subscale and the Competing subscale for the OCCI and the TKI respectively had the lowest values for both the pre- and post-workshop tests. This profile is not just true for the study sample. The results of the data we gathered from the group of teaching assistants in the three-day mandatory orientation were remarkably similar to those of the study sample (*see Fig. 4.3*).

The qualitative data are also consistent with the view that, as styles for conflict management and conflict prevention, avoidance and accommodation are preferred over more competitive options. This conclusion is consistent with recent studies of international graduate students (Zweibel *et al.,* 2008) and faculty and medical residents (Adrian-Taylor *et al.,* 2007). It was also evident that the focus group participants were keenly aware of the power differential that permeates all interactions between students and their advisors. However, they also provided insights about the many demands and challenges faced by their faculty advisors. This empathy may reflect the emphasis of the workshop on becoming aware of faculty interests and the importance of considering the perspective of the faculty member when planning a meeting or during conversations. The students' awareness of the power differential between themselves and their advisors, coupled with the perceived importance of the relationship, may partially explain why avoidance and accommodating strategies are most often used by graduate students to prevent or manage conflict with their faculty advisors.

Interestingly, the focus group participants reported using avoidance strategies in a planned and proactive fashion, which appears to minimize conflicts with their advisors.

One hypothesis to explain the mismatch between our findings and the anecdotal reports about students' tendencies to adopt competing strategies is based on the extensive literature on the effects of anger on behavior and decision making (Lerner and Keltner 2000; Lerner and Tiedens 2006). It is common to find that students bring with them a history of avoiding and accommodating in their interactions with their advisors, often accompanied by accumulated resentment, when they adopt a positional style. What gets them to act is frequently a particular event or interaction with their advisor that triggers anger. In contrast to other negative emotions, anger drives goal-oriented behaviors (Lerner and Keltner 2000). This may be the reason for a departure from more passive options, such as avoiding and accommodating, in favour of a competing or positional style. Anger also affects cognition and decision making; it increases an individual's optimism about potential risks associated with a course of action (*e.g.*, a particular position) (Lerner and Keltner 2000). Given this, what conflict mediators report may be more germane to impulsive action due to anger than to the style of conflict management used by graduate students most of the time. Recommendations for modifying the workshop that stem from these observations are to devote less time to examining the positional approach and more to evaluating the benefits and risks of avoiding and accommodating strategies and to include a discussion of the effects of anger on negotiation skills and decision making (Lerner and Keltner 2000).

This study also examined if participating in the workshop affected the preference of the participants for conflict management styles. Consistent with the goals of the workshop, participants showed a trend towards a statistically significant increase in their preference for collaborative skills post-workshop as measured by the appropriate subscale of the TKI. The interest-based approach, which is endorsed by the content of the workshop, specifically promotes techniques to identify and emphasize opportunities for mutual gains through cooperation. Even though participating in the workshop promoted the use of more collaborative approaches, the qualitative data clearly indicates that many of the students continued the use of avoidance and accommodation when interacting with their faculty advisors. These patterns are similar to those reported in Watt's (1994) study, which was an evaluation of a college conflict resolution course. He concluded that after taking the class, individuals shifted toward a preference for using a collaborative management style but that they also continued to use competing and compromising styles.

On the OCCI measure there were no trends towards any differences for any of the three subscales. The lack of significant change in the OCCI solution orientation subscale could be due to the fact that this subscale concurrently measures collaboration and compromising. While the workshop promotes collaboration, the workshop content also suggests that a compromise between two positions is rarely the optimal outcome. Participating in the workshop may affect compromising and collaborating tendencies in opposite ways, thus negating any change in the composite measure. Another possibility for the limited findings with the OCCI could be due to how this instrument is affected by desirability. For instance, Wilson and Waltman (1988) examined two types of social desirability of the OCCI and estimated that a minimum of 20 to 40 per cent of the variance in ratings of strategies is due to social appropriateness. Consequently, individuals are more likely to report using solution-oriented strategies even when that does not represent their actual behaviours in conflict situations, which would make the measure less sensitive to changes as a result of an intervention such as our workshop.

Finally one theme that emerged from the content analysis of the participants' comments was that of support from others when facing challenges. It was evident that students make use of relationships and multiple mentors to obtain resources and to understand their options. Although this was not a theme explored in the workshop, it helps to understand how students develop strategies to navigate the power differential of their relationships with their advisors and even their guidance or dissertation committees. Facilitating a discussion of this aspect of the student's experience could be a valuable addition to the content of the workshop.

Conclusion

In summary, consistent with findings from earlier evaluations of this workshop (Klomparens and Beck 2004; Klomparens *et al.* 2004), graduate students reported that they were introduced to skills that were likely to improve their relationships with faculty members. Our results indicate that graduate students are more inclined to use avoidance and accommodating strategies as compared to competing or positional ones when facing conflicts. Instances of positional approaches to conflict may represent situations in which anger is a dominant influence in students' behaviour. Taken together, our results show that a single intervention in the form of an interactive workshop can increase the use of collaborative strategies and effective communication skills. However, the effects were modest; and, even after the workshop, the use of avoidance and accommodation continued to be prevalent when students manage conflicts. This indicates the need for additional interventions, such as follow-up sessions, to reinforce and enhance the impact of our current workshop. Klomparens *et al.* (2008) provide a detailed discussion about additional intervention strategies. One important local impact of our pre-workshop results has been a modification of the content of the training session so as to focus the discussion more on the limitations of avoidance and accommodating strategies and less on the negative aspects of competitive strategies. Also, we now emphasize how anger can impede the use of collaborative, interest-based approaches when facing conflicts.

REFERENCES

1. Adrian-Taylor, S., Noels, K., & Tischler, K. (2007). Conflict Between International Graduate Students and Faculty Supervisors: Toward Effective Conflict Prevention and Management Strategies. *Journal of Studies in International Education*, 11(1), 90–117.
2. Austin, A. E. (2002). Preparing the Next Generation of Faculty. *The Journal of Higher Education*, 73(1), 94–121.
3. Aquinis, H., Nesler, M. S., Quigley, B. M., Lee, S. J., & Tedeschi, J. T. (1996). Power Bases of Faculty Supervisors and Educational Outcomes for Graduate Students. *The Journal of Higher Education*, 67(3), 267–297.
4. Baird, L. L. (1995). Helping Graduate Students: A Graduate Advisor's View. In A. S. Pruitt-Logan & P. D. Isaac (Eds.), Student services for the Changing Graduate Student Population. *New Directions for Student Services*, 72 (pp. 25–32). San Francisco, CA: Jossey-Bass.
5. Blake, R., & Mouton, J. (1964). The *Managerial Grid*. Houston, TX: Gulf.
6. Bryman, A., & Cramer, D. (2005). *Quantitative Data Analysis with SPSS 12 and 13*. New York, NY: Routledge.
7. Cohen, C. M., & Cohen, S. L. (2005). *Lab Dynamics: Management Skills for Scientists*. Cold Spring Harbor, NY: Cold Spring Harbor Laboratory Press.
8. Creswell, J. (1994). *Research Design: Qualitative and Quantitative Approaches*. Thousand Oaks, CA: Sage.
9. Crowne, D. P., & Marlowe, D. (1964). *The Approval Motive*. New York, NY: Wiley.
10. Damrosch, D. (1995). *We Scholars: Changing the Culture of the University*. Cambridge, MA: Harvard University Press.
11. Deen, M. Y. (2000). Differences in the Solution-oriented Conflict Style of Selected Groups of 4-H Youth Development Volunteer Leaders. *Journal of Extension*, 38(1), 2000. Retrieved June 27, 2009, from http:// www.joe.org/joe/2000february/rb5.html
12. Fisher, R., & Ury, W. (1991). Getting to Yes: Negotiating Agreement Without Giving in. New York, NY: Penguin Books. Golde, C. (2000). Should I Stay or Should I Go? Student Descriptions of the Doctoral Attrition Process. *The Review of Higher Education*, 23(2), 309–332.
13. Golembiewski, R., Billingsley, K., & Yeager, S. (1976). Measuring

Change and Persistence in Human Affairs: Types of Change Generated by OD Designs. *The Journal of Applied Behavioural Science*, 12(2), 133–157.

14. Green, S. G., & Bauer, T. N. (1995). Supervisory Mentoring by Advisors: Relationships with Doctoral Student Potential, Productivity, and Commitment. *Personnel Psychology*, 48(3), 537–561.
15. Hall, J. (1969). Conflict Management Survey: A Survey on One's Characteristic Reactions to and Handling of Conflicts Between Himself and Others. Conroe, TX: Teleometrics International.
16. Harnett, R. T., & Katz, J. (1977). The Education of Graduate Students. *Journal of Higher Education*, 48(6), 646–664.
17. Holton, S. A. (1998). New Directions for Higher Education: Conflict Management in Higher Education. Boston, MA: Anker Publishing.
18. Johnson, L. W. (1992). The Effects of Conflict Management Training upon the Conflict Management Styles of Teachers. *Unpublished Doctoral Dissertation*, Gonzaga University, Washington, DC.
19. Keltner, J. W. (1998). Views from Different Sides of the Desk. In S. A. Holton (Ed.), Mending the Cracks in the Ivory Tower (pp. 164–191). Bolton, MA: Anker.
20. Klomparens, K., & Beck, J. (2004). Michigan State University's Conflict Resolution Programme: Setting Expectations and Resolving Conflict. In D. H. Wulff & A. E. Austin (Eds.), *Paths to the Professoriate* (pp. 250–263). San Francisco, CA: Jossey-Bass.
21. Klomparens, K., Beck, J., Brockman, J., & Nunez, A. (2008). *Setting Expectations and Resolving Conflicts in Graduate Education*. Washington, DC: Council of Graduate Schools.
22. Klomparens, K., Beck, J., Larson, R. S., & Brockman, J. (2004). *Setting Expectations and Resolving Conflicts in Graduate Education*. Journal for Higher Education Strategists, 2(1), 21–37.
23. Lerner, J. S., & Keltner, D. (2000). Beyond Valence: Toward a Model of Emotion-specific Influences on Judgment and Choice. *Cognition and Emotion*, 14(4), 473–493.
24. Lerner, J. S., & Tiedens, L. Z. (2006). Portrait of the Angry Decision Maker: How Appraisal Tendencies Shape Anger's Influence on Cognition. *Journal of Behavioural Decision Making*, 19(2), 115–137.
25. Lewicki, R., Barry, B., Saunders, D., & Minton, J. (2003). *Negotiation* (4th ed.). New York, NY: McGraw Hill.
26. Lovitts, B. E. (2001). *Leaving the Ivory Tower: The Causes and Consequences of Departure from Doctoral Study*. Lanham, MD:

Rowman and Littlefield.

27. Lovitts, B. E. (2004). Research on the Structure and Process of Graduate Education. In D. H. Wulff & A. E. Austin (Eds.), *Paths to the Professoriate* (pp. 115–136). San Francisco, CA: Jossey-Bass.
28. Mikheev, C. C. (2006). A Conflict Resolution Intervention's Effect on Adolescents' Rates of Peer Victimization and Conflict Strategy Use. *Unpublished doctoral dissertation*, The Graduate School of Arts and Sciences, Columbia University, New York, New York.
29. Nerad, M., & Miller, D. (1996). Increasing Student Retention in Graduate and Professional Programmes. In J. G. Haworth (Ed.), Assessing Graduate and Professional Education: Current Realities, Future prospects. *New Directions for Institutional Research*, 92 (pp. 61–76). San Francisco, CA: Jossey-Bass.
30. Patton, M. Q. (1990). Qualitative Evaluation and Research Methods (2nd ed.). Newbury Park, CA: Sage.
31. Putnam, L. L., & Wilson, C. E. (1982). Communicative Strategies in Organizational Conflicts: Reliability and Validity of a Measurement scale. In M. Burgoon (Ed.), *Communication Yearbook*, 6 (pp. 629–652). Newbury Park, CA: Sage.
32. Rahim, M. A. (1983). A Measure of Styles of Handling Interpersonal Conflict. *Academy of Management Journal*, 26(2), 368–376.
33. Rashid, J. W. (2001). Leadership Development: Conflict Management for College Student Leaders. *Unpublished Doctoral Dissertation*, Higher Education Administration, North Carolina State University, Raleigh, North Carolina.
34. Rubin, J., Pruitt, D., & Kim, S. H. (1994). *Social Conflict: Escalation, Stalemate and Settlement* (2nd ed.). New York, NY: McGraw Hill.
35. Sandy, S., Boardman, S., & Deutsch, M. (2006). Personality and Conflict. In M. Deutsch, P. Coleman, & E. Marcus (Eds.), *The Handbook of Conflict Resolution* (pp. 23–42). San Francisco, CA: Jossey-Bass.
36. Thomas, K. W., & Kilmann, R. H. (1974). *Thomas-Kilmann Conflict MODE Instrument*. Tuxedo, NY: Xicom.
37. Van de Vliert, E. (1997). *Complex Interpersonal Conflict Behaviour: Theoretical Frontiers*. East Sussex, UK: Psychology Press.
38. Van de Vliert, E., & Kabanoff, B. (1990). Toward Theory-based Measures of Conflict Management. *Academy of Management Journal*, 33(1), 199–209.
39. Wade-Benzoni, K., Rousseau, D., & Li, M. (2006). Managing

Relationships Across Generations of Academics. *International Journal of Conflict Management*, 17(1), 4–33.

40. Watt, W. M. (1994, November). Conflict Management: Using the Thomas-Kilmann Conflict Mode Instrument to Assess Levels of Learning in the Classroom. *Paper presented at the annual meeting of the Speech Communication Association*, New Orleans, LA.
41. Wilson, S. R., & Waltman, M. S. (1988). Assessing the Putnam-Wilson Organizational Communication Conflict Instrument (OCCI). *Management Communication Quarterly*, 1(3), 367–388.
42. Womack, D. F. (1988). Assessing the Thomas-Kilmann Conflict MODE Survey. *Management Communication Quarterly*, 1(3), 321–349.
43. Zweibel, E., Goldstein, R., Manwaring, J., & Marks, M. (2008). What Sticks: How Medical Residents and Academic Healthcare Faculty Transfer Conflict Resolution Training from the Workshop to the Workplace. *Conflict Resolution Quarterly*, 25(3), 321–350.

Developing a Human Capital Management Strategy

DEVELOPING HUMAN RESOURCE MANAGEMENT STRATEGY

Human Resource Management (HRM) has already emerged as a separate discipline to personnel. In personnel management, people management strategy is developed through a process that is separate to the development of the business strategy and in which the primary focus of attention and effort is within the HR function and on the current state. In HRM, people management strategy links to and cascades from the business strategy. It looks forward from the current state, focusing on making incremental changes to the way people are currently managed in order to implement the objectives in the annual business plan.

The HRM strategy is developed based upon a diagnosis comparing the way people are currently being managed against the requirements of the new business plan. It deals with key issues about people management, such as whether the organization should buy in or build its own talent. Once the strategy has been developed, these activities then need to be followed by implementation and evaluation and reporting.

The shaded areas in the following diagrammed illustrate a typical process for developing HRM strategy:

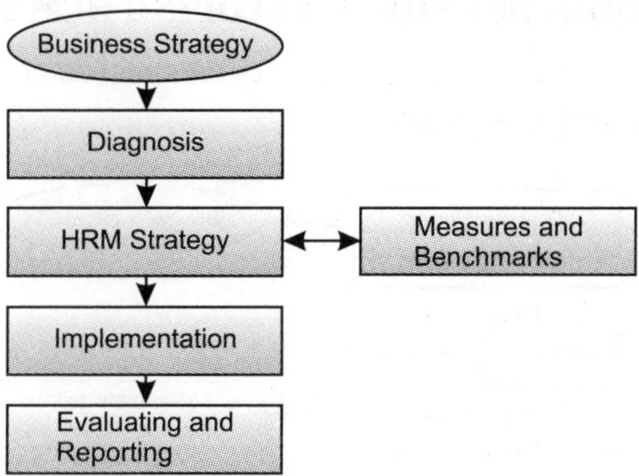

THE NEED FOR HUMAN CAPITAL MANAGEMENT

Moving up from personnel management to HRM strategy has served many organisations well. However, in today's business environment, organisations need to make transformational rather than incremental improvements in their products, services and the way they operate and manage their businesses. A strategic approach to human capital management (HCM) responds to this requirement by focussing on people's current and potential skills and abilities as a source of human capital and organisational transformation. HCM goes beyond just adding value to the business by supporting the delivery of business objectives for today. Instead it is about creating value by developing capability which can sustain and transform an organisation over the longer term.

This capability provides the basis for delighting an organisation's stakeholders, such as a company's investors, and which is the reason why a company's market worth can be so much more than just its book value. The focus here is on the future state, looking at what needs to be different and then working backwards from this future position. This results in more transformational and innovative approaches to people management than HRM's focus on the current state. So, how does the development of HCM strategy differ from the process provided earlier for HRM?

A METHODOLOGY FOR DEVELOPING HCM STRATEGY

The following diagrammed illustrates the main stages involved in developing an HCM strategy.

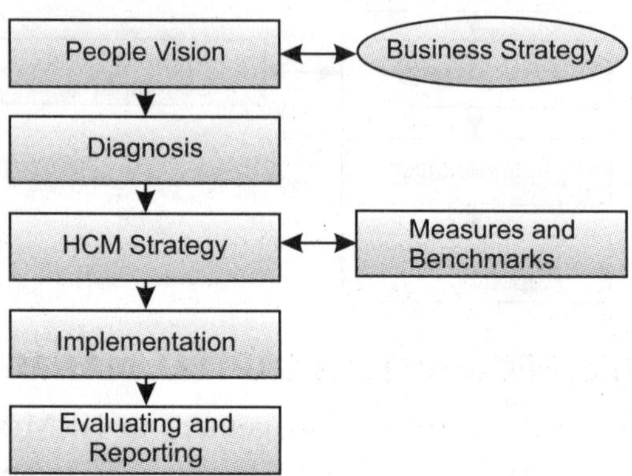

The key differences between this approach and the process used for developing HRM strategy are:

HCM Strategy Starts with a People Vision, Not Just the Business Strategy

The people vision focuses on the future and describes what might be possible based upon people's capability, or their potential capability.

The inputs into both the business strategy and the people vision include the organisation's mission, vision and values; the requirements of its customers, investors and other stakeholders; and any business trends, challenges and opportunities. Further inputs into the people vision include the current capability of the organisation; the capabilities of the organisation's competitors; workforce changes and opportunities; and line managers' and employees' perspectives about people and people management in the organisation. And as discussed in the following point, the business strategy and people vision are also informed by each other.

The Business Strategy and People Vision are tightly Integrated with Each Other

HCM strategy development is tightly integrated with development of the business strategy. This ensures that the capability the organisation is developing is aligned with an organisation's needs: its vision, mission, values and strategy. But this requirement for integration does not just mean that the people management strategy should simply support and align with the business strategy. It also means that at least on some occasions and for at least some of the time, the business strategy should be informed by the people management strategy rather than solely the other way around.

Diagnosis is Against the Future State People Vision

In HRM, diagnosis compares current people management activities to what may be required to implement the business strategy. It is grounded in the current state. In HCM, diagnosis focuses on the potential capability of the people working in the organisation and the gap between this and their current capability. It is therefore focussed on output rather than activity, and on the future, rather than the current state.

Innovative Strategy Development

HCM strategy deals with bigger and more strategic questions than within HRM. HCM requires innovative, unique, best fit approaches that go beyond current best practices to ensure human capital is developed is a way that is right for a particular organisation at a particular point in time. After all, investors are not going to pay for human capital that is the same as every other organisation's. They want to see capability linked to an organisation's particular strategy, its differentiation and its competitive advantage.

London Business School professor, Lynda Gratton, calls these innovative, best fit approaches, signature processes, or more appropriately, signature experiences (2007), and emphasises the additional benefits they have in helping people figure out what the organisation is about, and providing them with meaning in their work. One of her examples is BP's peer challenge / peer assist process which has helped brings five previously independent oil companies together. In this process, business unit heads are required to exchange ideas and information with other heads within a peer group. To encourage this to happen, these managers' bonuses are paid depending upon the performance of the whole group.

It is important to note that another related change between the development of HRM and HCM strategy is that whilst HRM typically involves a very analytical, left brained approach, HCM strategy development requires the use of much more creative thinking. This can supply ideas and insights that linear, logical thinking cannot provide and it opens up new opportunities that lie outside existing mindsets. After all, when people think like they have always thought, they tend to get what they have always got.

MEASUREMENT IN HCM STRATEGY DEVELOPMENT

Setting Strategic Measures

Once an HCM strategy has been developed, measures can be selected to support the management of this strategy. These measures should refer to the nature and level of human capital within the organisation, but also to the other elements of the HCM value chain: the initial inputs and investments the organisation is making in HCM; the processes or activities which the organisation is implementing to develop its human capital; and the impacts of this development on an organisation's business processes, its customers and financial results.

A relevant example that is included in my book (Ingham, 2006) is the BBC's evaluation of its five year, £5,000 per head leadership development programme which is a compulsory requirement for the BBC's 7000 managers. The programme aims to develop an intangible capability: creative leadership, which will support the BBC's ongoing effectiveness during a period of dramatic change.

The programme blends a rich mix of development activities including 360 degree feedback, group sessions, real-life assignments, coaching, action learning and relearning, including an online leadership wiki. The BBC evaluates the programme at each level in the HCM value chain:

- *Input:* What is the programme delivering, when is being delivered, who is it being delivered to, how much is it costing?
- *Activity:* What is the reaction to the programme? Is it relevant to people's roles? Can people use it in their jobs?
- *Output (human capital):* Have skills and knowledge improved? Has there been observable behaviour change / performance improvement? What is the business climate for supporting transfer?
- *Business impact:* What is the change to business performance? What is the change to organisation culture?

Benchmarking

Benchmarking helps ensure that measures have been set to be appropriately stretching, and can also generate new ideas and innovations. One type of benchmarking focuses on metrics measuring the effectiveness and efficiency of people management processes, and the other type focuses on the processes themselves. Metrics based benchmarking focuses on 'what' other companies have achieved. Knowing this can help raise aspirations about what might be possible and it provides objective data that can be useful in convincing sceptics of the need to change. However, potentially more value can be obtained by focusing on 'how' other organisations have achieved their results. In this process-based approach, organisations can benchmark their own approach to HCM with that of another organisation. Most often, this involves benchmarking a particular process with the same process in one or more benchmark organisations within the same sector. More risk but potentially greater benefits are involved in benchmarking against the same process in a different sector, or against a different process.

Process benchmarking is often done on a reciprocal basis but it can be done covertly too. At one client I was involved with, the client wanted to study the recruitment processes of five other leading companies it had already identified. We identified people we knew who had previously worked in one of these organisations or had otherwise been touched by their recruitment processes, for example having unsuccessfully applied to join. We were able to uncover a lot of information about the five companies' processes.

THE METHODOLOGY IN PRACTICE

To be effective, HCM strategy development needs to involve a broad spectrum of business leaders. One useful approach for doing this is a three-day, large-scale, facilitated event in which highly energised collaboration can take place. The event consists of a large group planning meeting that brings together a diverse group of stakeholders who are concerned with the way people provide value to an organisation. Participants could include the CEO; other Board members; the leadership team; HR, Finance, IT and other functions; line managers; core talent representatives; other talent pools especially young people to balance what is likely to be a fairly senior group; customers and key shareholders; preferred suppliers of people management services, outsourcing partners and thought leaders connected with the organisation. HR professionals are facilitators of the process, not owners of all of the results.

First Day : Understanding

The objective on the first day is to build a common database where everyone has had the same sort of information and has had the chance to discuss and question this information with people from other stakeholder groups. As much as possible, data should focus on the future. Anticipated customer and labour market trends are likely to be more useful than analysis of historic trends within the organisation. Information should also balance metrics and benchmarks with anecdotes and stories.

These can be gathered from across the organisation before the event, and may be presented as video diaries and in other emotionally rich forms. External speakers may also be used. Information should include the business' and its competitors' strategies; existing people and organisational capability; the external customer, investor and talent marketplaces; and broader people issues including demographic trends and cultural changes.

Second day: Creating a People Vision

The objective of the second day is to think creatively about future possibilities. It is useful to start with some creative thinking exercises. The main part of the day can consist of an open-space forum in which people are able to suggest the areas they want to work on to meet the challenges discussed on the first day. The only constraint on these groups is that they have to help in imagining the capabilities the organisation will need about five to ten years into the future. Groups can generate ideas and examples about their chosen future; and the barriers and enablers that may be encountered in the journey of getting there.

At the end of the day, people come back together to share the ideas that have been generated. After small group discussions, people prioritise the ideas, using post-its to note down what they agree and disagree with, and what questions they still have. Senior managers take these notes away for some evening work and come back the next day ready to present their conclusions about the final people vision they have agreed to.

Third Day: Strategy Development

At the start of the third day, managers present their conclusions, answer questions and respond to areas of disagreement. Measures are identified for the human capital and other outputs making up the people vision, and for the potential business impacts of these outputs. People then get into groups to work on the areas they are most interested in. Each group is tasked with creating a multi-mind mind map in which the central theme focuses on an aspect of the people vision. Some of the branches will relate to the impacts of these outputs, that is what the organisation will be able to do differently as a result of these capabilities, and other branches will relate to the actions that the organisation needs to execute to develop these capabilities. Measures for activities and inputs also need to be identified.

The final stage in the process is preparing each of the programs for communication. Each mind map needs to be unpacked into an HCM value matrix (Ingham, 2006) and visual and compelling communications prepared to cascade the strategy to the rest of the organisation.

CONCLUSION

HCM strategy is best developed through a facilitated and creative process which starts with the development of a people vision and leads on, through diagnosis, to the development of the strategy and associated measures and benchmarks. This HCM strategy extends well beyond HR's current agenda and provides a basis for creating value through people and providing ongoing competitive advantage.

REFERENCE

1. Ingham, J. (2006). Strategic Human Capital Management: Creating Value Through People. Butterworth Heinemann.

Index

U

W

X